NASHA MUKT NAVNIRMAN

Awakening the Youth for National Reconstruction

Dr. Rohit Rastogi

notionpress.com

INDIA · SINGAPORE · MALAYSIA

ISBN
Paperback 979-8-90342-679-9
Hardcase 979-8-90392-620-6

Disclaimer

This book is a compilation of data, reports, research publications, and materials available in the public domain. While due care has been taken in its preparation, the author makes no representation or warranty regarding the accuracy or completeness of the information provided.

The content is intended solely for educational and informational purposes and does not constitute legal, medical, psychological professional advice.

All stories, case studies, names, characters, institutions, and locations mentioned are fictional or used illustratively. Any resemblance to actual persons, living or deceased, or to real events is purely coincidental and unintended. No reference is intended to any specific individual, community, caste, creed, religion, or organization.

The author shall not be held liable for any direct or indirect loss, damage, or consequences arising from the use or interpretation of the contents of this book.

Dedication

To every young person fighting this invisible epidemic, and to the thousands of Master Volunteers and NGO workers who dedicate their lives towards lighting the path to recovery.

Contents

About the Author

Dr. Rohit Rastogi

Author - Nasha Mukt Navnirman

Dr. Rohit Rastogi is an academic leader, education strategist, and social reform advocate with over 20 years of experience in higher education and institutional development. His journey reflects a deep commitment to academic excellence, youth empowerment, and nation-building.

An alumnus of XLRI Jamshedpur, he further strengthened his expertise through the Train the Trainer program at IIT Roorkee and participated in the Industry-Academic University Partnership program at Dubai Knowledge Park, gaining international exposure in higher education collaboration.

During his leadership journey, he has held key positions at various educational institutions and is currently serving as the Founding Registrar of DBS Global University, Dehradun. In this role, he oversees academic governance, regulatory compliance, quality assurance, accreditation, branding, and strategic growth initiatives, significantly strengthening institutional positioning and outreach.

Beyond administration, he remains actively engaged in youth mentoring and social awareness initiatives. Nasha Mukt Navnirman draws from his two decades of experience with students and society, combining research insights and real-life narratives to promote a drug-free and responsible India.

Dr. Rastogi is a member of Association of MBAs (AMBA) and a lifetime member of the Federation of World Academics, underscoring his commitment to global academic excellence and social transformation.

"A drug-free mind is the first act of nation-building."

Acknowledgements

Writing this book, "Nasha Mukt Navnirman," has been a journey of deep reflection and collective hope. While the words on these pages are mine, the vision was made possible through the unwavering support of many. I would like to extend my deepest gratitude to three individuals whose contributions were pivotal in bringing this work to life:

- **Lt Gen Gurmit Singh, PVSM, UYSM, AVSM, VSM (Retd),**

  Honourable Governor of Uttarakhand

  For your tireless dedication to the cause of youth empowerment. Your insights into community resilience provided the intellectual foundation this book needed, and your motivational thoughts at Chitan Shivir kept me focused during the most challenging chapters.

- **Mr Akash Belwal**: *For being the bridge between theory and creative story writing. Your on-ground experience and the stories you shared from the heart of our communities gave this book its soul and its urgency.*

- **Dr Abdal Ahmed**: *For your meticulous editorial guidance and belief in this project from day one. You helped transform a collection of ideas into a cohesive roadmap for a drug-free India.*

To these three, my family and the many others who stood by me, I offer my sincerest thanks. This book belongs to everyone who believes in a healthier, empowered future for our nation.

Short Introduction of the Book:

The Cost of Silence

I grew up believing that drug abuse was a problem of the marginalized, the distant slums, the border towns. It wasn't until I saw a friend, a bright, ambitious engineering student, trade his textbooks for a syringe that I understood the epidemic respects no class or boundary. It is a silent predator that thrives in the shadows of our social structures, often fueled by the very silence we maintain out of shame or denial.

This book, "Nasha Mukt Navnirman," is born from that realization. It is not just a clinical analysis or a compilation of data; it is a declaration. It is a testament to the fact that the fight against substance abuse in India requires far more than top-down policies or legal frameworks. While legislation provides the skeleton, the lifeblood of this struggle must be a mass movement fueled by empathy, led by our youth, and grounded in the bedrock of community resilience.

The statistics are sobering, but they do not tell the whole story. The true cost is found in the hollowed-out potential of a student, the fractured peace of a family, and the weakened pulse of a community. We stand at a critical juncture where India's "demographic dividend" could either be our greatest strength or our most tragic vulnerability.

We, the generation most affected by this crisis, must also be the generation that ends it. This requires us to transform from passive observers into active architects of a new social fabric, one where a young person's worth is celebrated, where mental health is prioritized, and where "resilience" is a shared community practice rather than a solo burden.

The title Navnirman signifies a "new construction." It is an invitation to rebuild. As you turn these pages, I hope you see not just the challenges we face, but the immense power we hold when we stand together. The future of India is being written today in our classrooms, our villages, and our digital spaces. We must ensure it is written with a steady hand, a clear mind, and a heart that is unequivocally drug-free.

LT GEN GURMIT SINGH
PVSM, UYSM, AVSM, VSM (Retd)
GOVERNOR UTTARAKHAND

सत्यमेव जयते

LOK BHAWAN
UTTARAKHAND
Phone : 0135-2757400
2757403

19 March, 2026

Message

I am pleased to learn about the publication of the book "Nasha Mukt Navnirman," which seeks to promote awareness and collective responsibility towards building a drug-free, healthy, and progressive society.

Substance abuse remains one of the serious challenges facing our society today, particularly affecting the youth who represent the strength and future of our nation. Addressing this issue requires sustained social awareness, value-based education, and active participation from institutions, communities, and families. Initiatives such as this publication play an important role in encouraging dialogue, understanding the social and moral dimensions of substance abuse, and inspiring individuals to contribute towards a healthier and more responsible society.

By bringing together reflections, experiences, and insights on anti-drug initiatives, the book reinforces the spirit of collective action envisioned under the Nasha Mukt Bharat Abhiyan. Our young generation must be guided by strong values, positive aspirations, and a sense of responsibility towards society and the nation.

I commend the efforts of the author and all those associated with this initiative for contributing to the important cause of social awareness and nation building.

My best wishes for the success of this publication and hope that it will inspire many to actively participate in the mission of building a Nasha-Mukt Bharat.

Gurmit

Lt Gen Gurmit Singh (Retd)

पुष्कर सिंह धामी

मुख्यमंत्री, उत्तराखण्ड

उत्तराखण्ड सचिवालय
देहरादून - 248001
फोन : 0135-2650433
0135-2716262
फैक्स : 0135-2712827
कैम्प कार्यालय
फोन : 0135-2750033
0135-2750344
फैक्स : 0135-2752144

संदेश

मुझे यह जानकर अत्यन्त प्रसन्नता हो रही है कि **डी0बी0एस0 ग्लोबल यूनिवर्सिटी** द्वारा **"नशा मुक्त नव निर्माण"** पुस्तक का प्रकाशन किया जा रहा है। यह प्रकाशन केवल एक पुस्तक नहीं, बल्कि समाज में जागरूकता, नैतिकता, स्वास्थ्य और सकारात्मक परिवर्तन की दिशा में एक सशक्त जन–अभियान का स्वरूप है। आज नशा एवं मादक पदार्थों का दुरुपयोग समाज, विशेषकर युवाओं के भविष्य के लिए गंभीर चुनौती बनकर उभरा है। यह न केवल व्यक्ति के स्वास्थ्य को प्रभावित करता है, बल्कि परिवार, समाज और राष्ट्र की प्रगति को भी बाधित करता है। ऐसे समय में "नशा मुक्त नव निर्माण" जैसी पुस्तक का प्रकाशन अत्यन्त प्रासंगिक, प्रेरणादायी एवं मार्गदर्शक है। यह पहल निश्चित रूप से समाज को नशामुक्ति के प्रति सजग करते हुए स्वस्थ एवं सशक्त राष्ट्र के निर्माण की दिशा में महत्वपूर्ण भूमिका निभाएगी। उत्तराखण्ड देवभूमि है, जहाँ की सांस्कृतिक परंपराएँ, नैतिक मूल्य एवं आध्यात्मिक चेतना सदैव समाज को सकारात्मक दिशा प्रदान करती रही हैं। हमारी युवा शक्ति राज्य और देश की सबसे बड़ी पूंजी है। यदि यह शक्ति नशे की प्रवृत्तियों से मुक्त होकर शिक्षा, कौशल, नवाचार और राष्ट्रनिर्माण में संलग्न होगी, तो हमारा भविष्य उज्ज्वल एवं सुरक्षित होगा। इस दृष्टि से यह पुस्तक युवाओं को प्रेरित करने, उन्हें सही दिशा देने तथा जीवन मूल्यों के प्रति जागरूक बनाने में अत्यन्त सहायक सिद्ध होगी। राज्य सरकार भी नशामुक्त समाज के निर्माण के लिए प्रतिबद्ध है। विभिन्न जागरूकता अभियानों, परामर्श सेवाओं, पुनर्वास कार्यक्रमों तथा युवाओं के लिए सकारात्मक अवसरों के सृजन के माध्यम से हम निरंतर प्रयासरत हैं। मुझे आशा है कि इस प्रकार के साहित्यिक एवं शैक्षिक प्रयास इन सरकारी पहलों को और अधिक प्रभावी बनाएँगे तथा समाज में सकारात्मक वातावरण का निर्माण करेंगे।

मेरी ओर से डॉ0 रोहित रस्तोगी जी एवं **डी0बी0एस ग्लोबल यूनिवर्सिटी** की पूरी टीम को "**नशा मुक्त नव निर्माण**" पुस्तक के सफल प्रकाशन के लिए हार्दिक बधाई एवं शुभकामनायें।

(पुष्कर सिंह धामी)

डॉ0 धन सिंह रावत,
मंत्री
चिकित्सा स्वास्थ्य, चिकित्सा शिक्षा,
सहकारिता, उच्च शिक्षा, संस्कृत
शिक्षा, विद्यालयी शिक्षा

उत्तराखण्ड सरकार

विधान सभा भवन
कक्ष संख्या : 20
फोन : 0135–2666410
फैक्स : 0135–2666411

संदेश

यह अत्यन्त हर्ष का विषय है कि डी0बी0एस0 ग्लोबल विश्वविद्यालय, देहरादून, उत्तराखण्ड द्वारा समाज में बढ़ती नशे की प्रवृत्ति के प्रति जन–जागरूकता एवं विशेष रूप से युवाओं को सकारात्मक दिशा प्रदान करने के उद्देश्य से "नशा मुक्त नव–निर्माण" शीर्षक से एक पुस्तक का संकलन किया जा रहा है।

मुझे पूर्ण विश्वास है कि यह पुस्तक नशा उन्मूलन से जुड़े सामाजिक, शैक्षणिक एवं स्वास्थ्यगत पहलुओं पर प्रकाश डालते हुये एक स्वस्थ, जागरूक एवं सशक्त समाज के निर्माण का संदेश देगी। साथ ही शिक्षा, स्वास्थ्य एवं सहकारिता जैसे महत्वपूर्ण क्षेत्रों में नशे की प्रवृत्ति को रोकने हेतु किये गये उपायों को भी इस पुस्तक में सम्मिलित किया जाना, समाज के लिये अत्यन्त प्रेरणादायी होगा।

मैं, इस पुस्तक के संकलन के लिए विश्वविद्यालय को अपनी ओर से बधाई एवं शुभकामनायें प्रेषित करता हूँ।

(डॉ धन सिंह रावत)

सुबोध उनियाल
मंत्री
SUBODH UNIYAL
Minister

उत्तराखण्ड सरकार

वन, तकनीकी शिक्षा, भाषा एवं निर्वाचन
उत्तराखण्ड सरकार, देहरादून-248 001
Forest, Technical Education
Language & Election
Govt. of Uttarakhand, Dehradun-248 001

MESSAGE

It gives me pleasure to know about the forthcoming book authored by Dr. Rohit Rastogi with a title "Nasha Mukt Navnirman", is likely to publish.

In fact, this is the outcome of long-time engagement of author in higher education, leadership and youth development. It brings together institutional experiences, policy reflections and field-based narratives addressing the growing concern of substance abuse among youth fraternity. Youths are strength of the nation. Substance abuse seepage across the semi-urban towns and rural localities is a point of worrisome.

This publication is centered to highlight the social, moral and developmental dimensions of substance abuse prevention, while encouraging institutions, families and policymakers to actively contribute towards building a 'Nasha Mukt Bharat'.

The collective responsibility of 'Nasha Mukt Bharat' is a good initiative for strengthening the efforts and hope it shall pave a way for the abuse prevention campaign.

I extend my good wishes for this social cause and also grand success for the publication.

Best Wishes

II Subodh Uniyal II

Dated : Dehradun
March 2nd, 2026.

Dr. Rohit Rastogi
Author – *Nasha Mukt Navnirman*
Registrar, DBS Global University
Dehradun, Uttarakhand.

कक्ष संख्या– 124–125, प्रथम तल, विधानसभा भवन, देहरादून – 248001
Room No.- 124 - 125, 1st Floor, Vidhan Sabha Bhavan, Dehradun- 248001, Uttarakhand
☎ +91 -135-2666671, +91- 135-2665855 (fax), Mail us to: ministryuk1@gmail.com

List of Acronyms

NMBA	Nasha Mukht Bharat Abhiyan
MoSJE	Ministry of Social Justice and Empowerment
NDDTC	National Drug Dependence Treatment Centre
AIIMS	All India Institute of Medical Sciences
NGO	Non-Governmental Organisation
NPS	Novel Psychoactive Substance
NDPS Act	Narcotic Drugs and Psychotropic Substances Act
UNODC	United Nations Office on Drugs and Crime
GDP	Gross Domestic Product
PWID	People Who Inject Drug
JEE	Joint Entrance Examination
NEET	National Eligibility Cum Entrance Test
ODICs	Outreach and Drop-in Centers
PFC	Prefrontal Cortex
IRCAs	Integrated Rehabilitation Centers for Addicts
NDDS	National Drug De-addiction Strategy
SEL	Social and Emotional Learning
MV	Master Volunteer
MET	Motivational Enhancement Therapy
DDCs	Drug De-addiction Centres
MAT	Medication-Assisted Treatment
NCB	Narcotics Control Bureau
NYKS	Nehru Yuva Kendra Sangathan
NSS	National Service Scheme
CBT	Cognitive Behavioral Therapy

RPP	Relapse Prevention Therapy
JJ	Juvenile Justice
CML	Critical Media Literacy
SUDs	Substance Use Disorders
NDRI	National Drug Research Institute

Part I

Understanding the Crisis

(The Reality)

CHAPTER 1

The Invisible Epidemic

1.1 The Shifting Contours of Substance Use in India

Substance abuse in India has historically been associated with traditional substances like opium derivatives and naturally occurring cannabis products. However, the last decade has seen a radical and alarming transformation, pushing the crisis out of the shadows and into the mainstream of urban and rural life. This shift is characterized by three main trends: the rise of **synthetic drugs**, the normalization of **polydrug use**, and the dangerous adoption of **inhalants by minors**.

The 2019 National Survey on Extent and Pattern of Substance Use, commissioned by the Ministry of Social Justice and Empowerment (MoSJE) and conducted by NDDTC, AIIMS, remains the baseline for understanding the scale, though NGO field reports suggest figures continue to rise, particularly post-pandemic.

The reality today is that India is a significant consumer *and* transit hub. Border States like Punjab, Mizoram, and Nagaland bear the immediate brunt of trafficking routes, but the internal crisis is now national.

Substance Category (Age 10-75)	Estimated Users (in Crores)	Percentage of Population (Approx.)
Alcohol	16.0	14.6%
Cannabis (Ganja, Charas, Bhang)	3.1	2.8%
Opioids (Heroin, Opium, Pharma)	2.2	2.1%
Sedatives (Non-medical use)	1.18	1.08%
Inhalants	0.63	0.58%

(Source: Magnitude of Substance Use in India, 2019, NDDTC, AIIMS & MoSJE)

1.2 The Rise of Synthetics and Pharmaceutical Diversion

The most challenging development is the proliferation of **Synthetic Drugs** and the non-medical use of pharmaceutical opioids and sedatives. These drugs are easier to conceal, cheaper to produce, and offer high potency, making them attractive to organized crime and youth looking for a quick, cheap 'high.'

- **Pharmaceutical Misuse:** Opioids like Tramadol, Codeine-based cough syrups, and sedatives like Alprazolam are diverted from legitimate supply chains. In certain regions, **40 lakh people** (4 million) in India are estimated to require help for Opioid use, representing a massive dependency crisis fueled by both illicit Heroin and diverted pharmaceuticals. This trend is particularly rampant in affluent areas where access to prescription pads is easier, or in low-income areas where pharmacy laws are poorly enforced.

- **Novel Psychoactive Substances (NPS):** These 'designer drugs' constantly change their chemical structure to bypass legal restrictions (like the NDPS Act). These are often sold online or through encrypted messaging apps, posing a unique challenge for law enforcement and making awareness generation difficult for NGOs.

1.3 The Global Perspective and Local Impact

Drug abuse is not just a health issue; it is a developmental roadblock. The UNODC estimates that the drug trade annually accounts for an economic loss that affects global GDP significantly. Locally, this translates into:

1. **Economic Drain:** Families spend nearly **50% of their mean monthly income** on drugs, pulling them into cycles of debt and poverty, as noted by early UNODC studies on treatment seekers.
2. **Public Health Crisis:** The rise of **People Who Inject Drugs (PWID)**, estimated at **8.5 lakh people** nationally, particularly in states like Punjab and Uttar Pradesh, has created severe secondary health crises, including the spread of HIV, Hepatitis C, and Tuberculosis due to needle sharing.
3. **Gendered Burden:** While drug use is overwhelmingly higher among men (97.2% of treatment seekers are male), the burden of care, financial ruin, and emotional trauma falls disproportionately on women and children in the family unit, as frequently highlighted by NGOs working with caregivers.

STORY 1

The Ordinary Road

There are two kinds of hunger Aarav's father taught him to recognize: the kind that asks for food, and the kind that asks for proof. The first is honest. The second never stops eating.

The train let Aarav off for the city that's gonna impact his life in an unprecedented way. Blue suitcase, mark sheets, and a middle-class family's single dream folded into his pocket. His mother packed laddoos; his father packed advice and two thousand rupees: "In case of some unexpected expense."Dehradun did not ask.

Pines. Quiet roads. A hostel near Rajpur Road smelling of camphor. First semester: high marks, some academic textbooks, Sunday walks to watch Mussoorie lights. He phoned home from rooftops and described the sky.

Then Sana is a sharp, funny, Haldwani girl. Library whispers became canteen laughter and gloves held together in winter. She pulled him into her world: Friday nights in Vikrant's room, four people on one bed, arguing about movie endings. Manish, the calm senior, always brought snacks and something extra.

It started with caffeine pills during exams. Everyone did it downing them with Red Bull at 3 a.m., fingers stained with highlighter ink. "Bro, it's just caffeine," Vikrant said. "Doctors take these during residency." When Aarav hesitated, Nisha laughed: "What, you want to fail? It's survival, not cheating."

He swallowed one. Then everyone went back to their notes like nothing happened. Normal, Smart, even.

After mid-terms, his rank slipped to seventh. His father's disappointed pause on the phone felt longer than the conversation.

That weekend, Vikrant's birthday: dim lights, loud music, everyone loose and laughing. Aarav sat stiff on the edge, the only one not dancing

"Dude, you're killing the vibe," Vikrant said, half-joking, half-serious.

Manish leaned in, voice low, friendly: "You're always in your head, bhai. Overthinking everything. Everyone here's tried it. It's not heroin, just something to help you breathe." He held out a white pill. "See Nisha? She was crying about her breakup last week. Now look at her."

Nisha was dancing, carefree, alive.

"Even Sana's done it," Manish added casually.

Aarav looked at her. She didn't deny it. Just shrugged, not pushing, not stopping him. The room felt warm with acceptance. He was the only one outside the circle.

His father's voice: *Don't follow the crowd off a cliff.*

But his father wasn't here. Hadn't felt the shame of being the boring one, the scared one, the one who couldn't just relax like everyone else.

"One time," Aarav said.

Manish grinned. "That's the spirit. You'll thank me."

For two hours, every worry waited outside. His body felt light. Sana's hand felt like the only true thing. Everyone looked at him differently, finally one of them. He promised himself it was one time.

But the next Friday, Vikrant asked, "You coming tonight?" The unspoken message: *Are you cool or not?*

He went. It became weekend. Then Wednesdays because "why wait for Friday?" Then Tuesday because Monday was brutal. Manish always had more never been pushy, just there. "For you, bhai. Friends' rate." Making him feel special. Chosen. Trusted.

"Your boy's loosening up," Vikrant told Sana, approvingly.

She smiled, but it didn't reach her eyes.

By winter, things shifted. Aarav started needing it, not wanting, needing. Without it, he felt wrong. Exposed. Classes felt longer. Conversations felt harder. He'd sit in lectures watching others, wondering: *Do they feel this heavy all the time? How do they manage?*

Sana grew quiet around him. She checked her phone more, laughed at basketball boy's jokes, someone with clean eyes and steady hands. She started saying no to Friday nights. "I have assignments." But he'd see her Instagram stories: out with others, smiling the way she used to smile with him.

"Why don't you come anymore?" he asked one day.

"It's not fun anymore, Aarav. It used to be movies and stupid debates. Now it's just... that."

"Everyone does it."

"Not everyone. And even if they did " She stopped herself. "You're different now. You're there but you're not there."

He wanted to argue, but Manish called. He had to meet him. The conversation could wait.

It never happened again.

One Friday, Manish was gone, "family emergency." The pills ran out. By Saturday evening, Aarav's skin felt too tight. By Sunday, he was pacing his room, checking his phone every five minutes. The need wasn't dramatic, no shaking, no vomiting. Just a growing wrongness, like he'd forgotten how to be comfortable in his own body.

He couldn't wait until Manish returned.

He asked Vikrant. Vikrant looked uncomfortable. "Bro, I don't have a connection. I just take what Manish shares."

Nisha avoided his eyes. "Maybe take a break? You've been doing it a lot."

They were pulling away. He could feel it. The circle is closing without him.

A junior whose name he didn't know saw him near the canteen, agitated, checking his phone. "Are you looking for stuff?" the boy asked quietly. "There's a guy. Bhola. Chai stall by the main gate. Evenings. Everyone knows him."

Everyone knows him. That should have been a warning.

Bhola didn't look dangerous. Mid-forties, neat shirt, soft voice, like someone's concerned uncle. He asked about Aarav's studies, nodded sympathetically. "Engineering. Tough course. A lot of pressure, no? Parents expect, society expects, you expect yourself to be perfect."

He slid a packet across. "Manish is a good boy. His friends are my friends. First time, student price." Then, standing, hand on Aarav's shoulder: "You call me anytime. I'm always near. Never far." A pause. "Don't make me come looking, beta."

Kindly said. A threat.

The packet lasted three days. Then he needed more. Bhola's prices went up, "supply issues, beta, you understand." But he was always available, always one call away, always with that same sympathetic voice: "I know it's expensive. Tell you what, take now, pay Friday. I trust you."

The debt started small. Then it wasn't small.

Sana stopped answering calls. Made excuses. He saw her hand on another boy's arm. When they finally met, she wore the scarf he'd gifted her.

"You're not the same person," she said. "You skip classes. You disappeared for three days. Your hands shake. I saw you with that man."

"It's not,"

"Don't lie." Tears spilled. "I can't watch you disappear."

She walked out. Two weeks later, the scarf was on the back of another boy's bike.

He learned how absence sounds: like traffic continuing, like laughter that doesn't include you.

He called Bhola that night.

Another temptation came: Manish's stock Telegram group. First profit ₹3,000 in a day. He sent ₹2,000 home when his father's scooter failed. Praise multiplied. He skipped classes "for the market," planned generosity for rising balances.

Then loss. A script fell. He averaged down. It fell more. By evening, no story made sense. Fees were due. He borrowed from a classmate, then a senior, then Bhola. "Advance," Bhola called it. The interest came later. "Good boy. Don't make me come looking."

To dull the noise, calls he couldn't answer, notices, the way people looked through him, he reached for more. A smoke. A swallow. Then needles because nothing else worked. The high didn't lift anymore; it just erased.

One evening by Sahastradhara, palms on the bridge rail, he counted exits: the shortcut (river, quiet, debts erased) and the climb (confessions, shame, small work). In the dark he saw his father cutting mangoes: "Don't hurry. Let it be itself."

He stepped back.

He called home and used sentences that had never lied. His father said only, "We start from where we are."

A week in a Rishikesh clinic, tremors like trains inside him. A counselor asked: "What was the high promise? What did it cost?"

Promises: Courage. Love. Sleep. Fewer expectations.

Costs: Fees. Friends. Grades. His mother's laugh. His name.

He learned the difference between craving and need, numbing and healing, rally and income.

With his father, he sat in a police station. A sub-inspector took notes. Not cinematic, just enough. A complaint. A plan. Signatures with shaking hands. A boundary in daylight.

College didn't forgive me. Scholarship gone. He repeated a semester. The warden's wife slipped extra roti into his tiffin mercy.

He stacked cartons at a medical store in the evenings. The pharmacist taught him medicine names, and insisted on tea breaks. On paydays he felt a different high steady, like a floor that doesn't move. He called his mother at 4 p.m. Walked Rajpur Road. Shaved again.

Sana passed once in traffic. Their eyes agreed: no trial. He stopped rehearsing blame.

Placements: not the glossy job he'd imagined, but one that paid on time. He sent money home less than dreams, more than expected. His mother's laugh returned, slow and skittish.

He spoke to juniors in hushed hostel rooms and college seminars not as a warning but as a witness. He told them what no one had told him:

How it starts: "Everyone's doing it. It's just to cope. You'll be fine. Don't be boring."

The invisible line: You don't see yourself cross it. One day you can say no. The next day, you can't remember when that changed.

The isolation: Your real friends start pulling away. The only ones left are the ones using with you. And they're not friends, they're co-passengers on the same sinking ship.

The debt: It starts as ₹500. Then ₹2,000. Then you're calculating how to eat and pay both Bhola and the mess bill. Then you're stealing from your roommate's drawer.

The dealer's playbook: They're nice at first. Patient. "I trust you, beta." They make you feel chosen. By the time you realize it's a trap, the door's already locked.

The shame: You stop calling home because you can't lie anymore, but you can't tell the truth either. You become a ghost in your own life.

A girl raised her hand: "But what if everyone in your group does it? What if saying no means being alone?"

Aarav leaned forward. "Then you find a different group. I know that sounds easy and it's not. Being alone is scary. But being trapped is scarier. The group that pressures you to hurt yourself isn't a group, it's a cage that looks like friendship."

"One number," he said. "Keep one number you can call before the night turns to the tunnel. Someone who isn't impressed by you. Someone who'll pick up at 3 a.m. Your uncool friend. Your annoying cousin. That one senior who talks too much about discipline. Anyone who'd rather you alive and boring than cool and gone."

A boy in the back, eyes down: "What if you've already started?"

"Tell one person today. Not tomorrow. Today. Report ordinary things: I ate. I slept. I opened a window. The small things are the whole thing."

A boy asked, "When did you feel safe?"

"When I could watch the river without negotiating. When a good day felt like chai that stayed warm."

On the bridge anniversary, he returned with his father. "You chose the climb," his father said.

"Every day," Aarav replied.

Driving back, he saw three paths: the shortcut, the climb, and the ordinary road that keeps going to tea stalls, rent due, juniors who need listening, work no one claps for, hills that stay whether you learn their names.

He took that road. Not because it was heroic. Because it led home.

What you can do next >>>

For Students	For Parents	For Teachers
Educate Yourself: Learn about "Gateway Drugs" (tobacco, alcohol) and how they prime the brain for harder substances.	**Look for "Invisible" Signs:** Monitor for non-disruptive changes like sudden secrecy, sleep shifts, or unexplained money loss.	**Map Vulnerability:** Identify students in high-stress "transition points" (e.g., preparing for JEE/NEET or moving to hostels).
Recognize Triggers: Identify if you are using substances to "self-medicate" for exam stress or anxiety.	**Normalize Mental Health:** Talk openly about stress and depression to remove the incentive for your child to use drugs as a "calmative".	**De-stigmatize Addiction:** Use the "Disease Model" in class to explain that addiction is a chronic brain disorder, not a moral failing.

CHAPTER 2

The Youth Vulnerability Map

2.1 Statistics: The Alarming Numbers for Minors

The focus of *Nasha Mukt Navnirman* is the youth demographic (10–25 years), the future workforce of India. Data confirms that this group is not only initiating drug use earlier but is also disproportionately vulnerable to certain categories of substances.

Focus on the 10–17 Age Group:

Substance	Estimated Children Users (10-17 years)	Percentage Prevalence
Inhalants	30,00,000 (30 Lakh)	1.17% (Highest compared to adult use)
Alcohol	30,00,000 (30 Lakh)	1.30%
Opioids	40,00,000 (40 Lakh)	1.80%

The most immediate danger is **Inhalant Use**. The survey showed that 1.17% of children use inhalants, significantly higher than the 0.58% adult prevalence. This trend is driven by accessibility, low cost (glue, paint thinners, gasoline), and a lack of social stigma regarding products found in every household or corner store. NGOs like CHILDLINE have repeatedly pointed out that street children often turn to inhalants as a form of self-medication to cope with hunger, cold, and violence.

2.2 Identifying High-Risk Environments

Vulnerability is geographically and contextually defined. A successful prevention strategy must map these high-risk zones, where the environment itself acts as a multiplier of risk.

a. Border States and Transit Routes (The Supply Front)

States along the "Golden Crescent" (Afghanistan, Pakistan, Iran) and the "Golden Triangle" (Myanmar, Laos, Thailand) face an existential threat.

- **Punjab and Jammu & Kashmir:** These states, historically and currently affected by cross-border trafficking, show some of the highest rates of **early initiation**. NGO rapid assessments in these regions often report that adolescents initiate drug use *before* the age of 15 at higher rates than the national average.
- **Northeast States (Mizoram, Nagaland):** These regions show unique usage patterns and a high proportion of young drug abusers (e.g., 37.9% of users below 20 years old in Mizoram in earlier reports), often driven by accessibility to international smuggling routes.

b. Urban Slums and Homeless Children (The Social Exclusion Front)

Street children and those in urban slum clusters face multi-layered abuse. NGOs working with these populations confirm that drug use is primarily a coping mechanism, not recreational choice.

- Lack of access to clean water, sanitation, and education.
- High rates of physical and sexual abuse.
- Poverty necessitates long working hours.

In these environments, organizations running **Outreach and Drop-In Centres (ODICs)** become lifelines, offering screening, counseling, and a pathway to rehabilitation that the formal system often misses.

c. Educational Institutions (The Peer Pressure Front)

Schools, colleges, and university campuses are ground zero for peer pressure and experimentation. The pressure cooker environment of competitive academics, combined with the sudden freedom of college life, can push vulnerable students towards substances as a stress reliever or a social lubricant.

- **Peer Influence:** Studies show that students are **10 times more likely** to use drugs if their close friends do. The key challenge for institutions is not just detection but fostering a culture where positive social norms outweigh negative peer pressure.

2.3 The Psycho-Social Risk Factors

The drug crisis among youth is intrinsically linked to underlying social and psychological factors. NGO counseling data consistently points to these drivers:

1. **Academic and Career Stress:** The intense pressure to clear competitive exams (JEE, NEET, Civil Services) often leads to anxiety, burnout, and depression. Many turn to sedatives (often non-prescribed) or alcohol to "calm nerves" or "aid focus," leading quickly to dependence.
2. **Parental and Familial Dysfunction:** Lack of parental communication, neglect, or parental substance abuse dramatically increases a child's risk. The absence of a stable,

supportive family environment compels youth to seek validation and escapism elsewhere.

3. **Media and Normalization:** The subtle or overt glamorization of substance use in popular culture, cinema, and music videos creates an illusion of coolness or sophistication, directly challenging preventative messaging.

2.4 The Student Lifecycle: Pathways to Vulnerability

The student experience in India is marked by distinct transition points, each introducing a surge in vulnerability to substance use due to changes in social pressure, academic demands, and supervision levels. Understanding these three critical stages is vital for targeted intervention.

a. Phase 1: Early Adolescence and Initiation (Ages 10-15)

This phase corresponds to middle school and early high school. Initiation is driven primarily by **curiosity, novelty, and accessibility**.

- **Substances of Choice:** Inhalants (glue, correction fluids, petrol), cheap tobacco products, and experimental use of alcohol (often sourced from home or through older siblings).
- **Triggers:**
    - **Low Parental Monitoring:** The child spends less time at home and more time in unsupervised peer groups.
    - **Peer Validation:** A desperate need to fit into a perceived 'tough' or 'cool' social group.
    - **Availability:** Easy access to inhalants from neighborhood shops due to their non-regulated nature.

b. Phase 2: Late Adolescence and Experimentation (Ages 16-18)

This phase spans the final years of high school and the intense preparation for competitive entrance exams. Use often shifts from mere curiosity to **stress relief and social lubrication**.

- **Substances of Choice:** Cannabis (Ganja, Charas), increased alcohol use (binge drinking), and the misuse of prescription sedatives (e.g., pain relievers, sleeping pills) for anxiety or sleep deprivation.
- **Triggers:**
    - **Academic Stress:** The pressure to perform in board exams or entrance tests (JEE, NEET) drives students to seek chemical shortcuts for relaxation or focus.
    - **Erosion of Family Time:** Intense study schedules mean less family connection, leaving emotional needs unmet.
    - **Financial Autonomy:** Teenagers often gain small amounts of pocket money or earn through part-time work, increasing purchasing power for illicit substances.

c. Phase 3: Young Adulthood and Habituation (Ages 18-25)

This phase includes university life, moving away from home (hostel life), and beginning career exploration. This stage is characterized by **unsupervised freedom and performance demands**.

- **Substances of Choice:** Opioids (often diverted pharmaceuticals like Tramadol/Codeine), potent cannabis derivatives, and, increasingly, **Novel Psychoactive Substances (NPS)** available through college networks.
- **Triggers:**

- **Newfound Freedom:** The lack of immediate parental control in hostels and PGs leads to reckless experimentation and unmonitored peer environments.
- **Performance Enhancement:** Misuse of pharmaceuticals (colloquially called 'smart drugs' or sedatives) to stay awake for long periods or manage presentation anxiety, rapidly leading to dependency.
- **Isolation and Identity Crisis:** Failure in competitive exams or disillusionment with course choices can lead to depression, with substance use becoming a primary coping mechanism for existential pain.

This lifecycle model underscores the need for prevention strategies that are specifically tailored to the unique psychological and environmental stressors present at each educational checkpoint.

Layered Risk Model

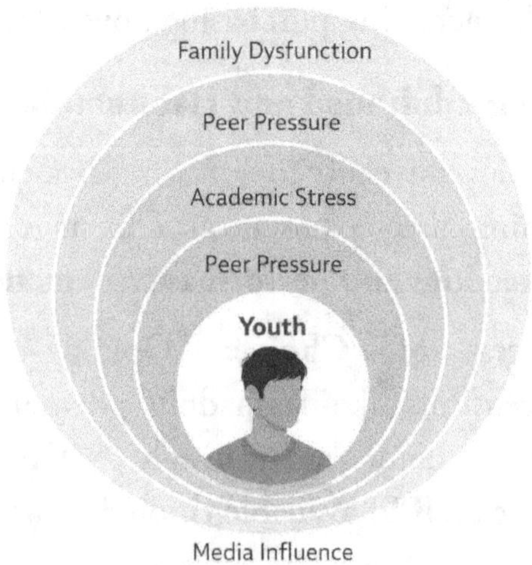

STORY 2

The Fortress

There are two kinds of silence, Priya learned: the kind that holds space for words to come, and the kind that builds walls between people who live in the same house.

Her family practiced the second kind.

Part One: The Performance

The dinner table at the Sharma household in Gurgaon was a well-choreographed performance. Father scrolled through his phone. Mother served rotis mechanically. Arjun, her older brother, ate fast always somewhere else to be.

Priya, fifteen, pushed paneer around her plate and counted minutes until she could escape to her room. To her real life.

"Boards next year," her father said without looking up. "Mock test rank dropped to forty-seventh."

Not a question. Just a fact, delivered like a weather report.

"I'll work harder," Priya said. The script.

"Arjun was in the top ten throughout."

Arjun stood, plate half-full. "I have to go."

"Where?" Mother asked, but he was already gone. She didn't push. Hadn't pushed in years. The détente held: they didn't ask, he didn't lie.

Later, the group chat lit up:

Nandini: party at Ananya's. parents away. u coming?

Priya looked at her closed door. Her parents were in the living room, separated by the television's blue glow and whatever silence they'd built over twenty years. They wouldn't notice if she slipped out.

Priya: be there in 20

No one asked permission in her house. Permission required conversation.

Part Two: The Slip

Rhea came back from the bathroom with eyes like glass. "You have to try this. Japanese pills. Super safe. For studying. Makes everything easier."

"What is it?"

"Does it matter? It's not drugs-drugs. Not like that Dehradun guy remember Bhola? This is controlled. Everyone does it."

Priya hesitated.

"I'm not pushing. Just saying you looked miserable when you got here. Don't you want one night where your dad's voice isn't in your head?"

One night where forty-seventh didn't matter. Where the silence at dinner didn't sit on her chest.

"Just one," Priya said.

For three hours, her father's voice stopped. The math anxiety paused. The weird grief of watching her parents live like polite strangers is gone.

At 1 a.m., she climbed back through her window. Her parents' door was closed. Nobody asking, nobody knowing.

Part Three: The Slide

It's become weekend. Then Wednesdays. Then Tuesdays because Monday was unbearable.

Her mother noticed the late nights. "Where are you going?"

"Nandini's. Organic chemistry."

Her mother's eyes held the question for three seconds, then let it go. Asking more would require something neither of them knew how to do talk. Really talk.

So she nodded. And Priya understood: this was the family deal. Don't make us ask directly, and we won't look too closely.

By February, her rank was seventy-third. Her father's disappointment came in one sentence: "What's happening to you?"

Everything and nothing, she wanted to say. I'm drowning in the same house where you eat dinner.

"I'll fix it," she said instead.

That night she took more.

Part Four: The Breaking

Arjun found her at 2 a.m., bathroom floor, unable to stand. He'd come home drunk himself and heard her crying behind the locked door.

He picked the lock. Sat beside her while she shook.

"How long?" he asked.

"Four months."

"What are you taking?"

She told him. His jaw tightened. "Priya. That's not study pills."

"It helps."

"It doesn't help. It just makes you not care that nothing helps." His voice cracked. "Does anyone else know?"

"No. Don't tell Papa. He'll"

"Give you that look? The one that says you're not worth the investment anymore? I know that look. I've been getting it for five years." He looked at her. "I didn't tell anyone. And look at us. Two kids in the same house, both trying to disappear."

"What do you want me to do?"

"Tomorrow. Family dinner. You're going to tell them."

"Arjun, no"

"Or I will."

Part Five: The Conversation

Sunday dinner. Same table. But Arjun didn't let the silence settle.

"We need to talk. Actually talk. About Priya."

Their parents' eyes snapped to her.

"She's been using it," Arjun said. Flat. Direct. "Pills. Other stuff. Four months."

Sharp, airless silence.

"Using what?" their father said slowly.

Their father stood. "You're throwing your future away? After everything we"

"Satish, stop." Her mother's voice cut through.

He stopped. Stared at his wife.

She turned to Priya. "Are you okay? Right now are you safe?"

The question broke something. Priya started crying loud, ugly, from somewhere deeper than embarrassment.

"No. I'm not okay. I haven't been okay for months. And I didn't know how to tell you because we don't tell each other anything in this house."

Her mother moved fast, pulling Priya into her arms. When had they last hugged?

"Why didn't you tell us?" her mother whispered.

"When? During dinner when Papa's on his phone? When you ask about my marks but not why my hands shake? When everyone's just performing as a family?"

Her father sank into his chair. "We thought... you seemed fine."

"I'm fifteen. I don't know how to ask for help. That's supposed to be your job."

Arjun spoke: "I've been drinking since I was seventeen. Alone. In my room. None of you noticed until I stopped hiding it. Then we just stopped talking about it. About anything."

Their mother was crying. "When did we become strangers?"

"Slowly," Arjun said. "One quiet dinner at a time."

Part Six: The Rebuild

They called the NMBA helpline that night. The woman asked questions about what Priya was using, for how long, family support structure.

That last question hung.

"We're working on that," her mother said.

Dr. Mehra ran a family-centered program. The first session wasn't just for Priya for all of them.

"Substance use doesn't happen in a vacuum. We'll address Priya's usage, yes. But also why home didn't feel safe for her pain."

Her father looked uncomfortable. "We provided everything"

"Provisions aren't protection. Kids need emotional safety more than material comfort. They need to know they can fail and still be loved. Not loved if loved despite."

The sessions were hard. Safety plan: phone to mother by 8 p.m., no unsupervised outings for three months, regular tests.

But more than rules, they created rituals.

New dinner table: Phones in a basket. Mother asked: "What was the hardest part of your day?" Not marks your day.

Priya's first answer: "Sitting in chemistry and wanting to use it."

Her father's hand shook as he reached across. "Thank you for telling us."

They started small. Morning chai together. Friday movie Priya picked. Sunday walks, no destination.

Her mother learned the signs Dr. Mehra taught: dilated pupils, sudden secrecy, sleep changes. But more importantly: What are you really asking for?

When Priya came home stressed, instead of "Study harder," her mother tried: "That sounds overwhelming. Want to talk?"

The first few times, Priya didn't trust it. But her mother kept showing up. Keep listening without solutions, just presence.

Their father admitted: "I thought pushing you meant I cared. I didn't know it felt like rejection."

"It felt like we were projects," Arjun said. "Not people."

"You're my people. I'm sorry I forgot to show it."

Part Seven: The Relapse

Six weeks in, Priya relapsed. Exam stress. Message from Rhea: miss u, party Saturday?

She met the dealer. Took pills in the parking lot. I was home by dinner, eyes wrong.

Her mother saw immediately. "Priya?"

She could have lied. Three months ago, she would have.

"I used. Today. I'm sorry."

Her father started to stand then caught himself. Sat down. "Are you safe right now?"

How could you? But are you okay?

"Yes. It wasn't much. But I wanted to."

Her mother nodded. "We call Dr. Mehra. Right now. Together."

No screaming. No punishment. The protocol relapse isn't failure, it's information.

Dr. Mehra on speaker: "What triggered it?"

"Exam. Feeling like I wasn't enough."

"Did the pills make you not fail?"

"...No. They just made me not care."

"So what would actually help?"

Silence. Then: "Knowing it's okay if I don't come first. Knowing my parents won't look at me differently."

Her father's voice, rough: "Beta. I see you now. Not your rank. And I'm not going anywhere."

Part Eight: The Fortress

Recovery wasn't straight. There were hard days. But they kept showing up.

Her mother started a parents' support group. Her father started therapy to understand why achievement felt like the only language for love.

They established new rules:

Clear boundaries: "No substances. If you're struggling, tell us before you use it. We're your safety net, not your punishers."

Monitoring without surveillance: "I worry because I love you, not because I don't trust you."

One person at 3 a.m.: If Priya felt the pull, call mother first. No judgment just: "Stay on the phone. Let's get through five minutes."

She used it twice. Both times, it worked.

Eight months in, Priya spoke at her school's health class.

"I'm Priya. Sixteen. Eight months in recovery. You don't have to be broken to ask for help. You don't have to be failing to need someone."

A girl raised her hand. "What if your parents don't get it?"

"Then you try again. If they don't hear you, find someone else counselor, helpline, that one uncle who listens. Parents don't always know how to help. They're scared too. Sometimes you teach them how to reach you."

Another hand. "How do you know when it becomes a problem?"

"When you start planning your day around it. When you can't imagine feeling okay without it. When people who care feel like obstacles." She paused. "And if you're asking, you probably know."

Afterwards, her mother hugged her. "I'm proud of you."

"For recovering?"

"For surviving. For being braver than I was." Her mother looked away. "I had my own ways to cope. Nothing illegal, just silence, distance. I stopped telling my parents anything real at fourteen. Spent forty years thinking that was normal."

"What changed?"

"Almost losing you. Realizing I'd been so worried about being a 'good mother' that I forgot to be a real one."

Part Nine: Forward

A year later, the dinner table was different. They knew each other now. Not performances of real versions. The ones who struggled and failed and tried again.

Her father learned to say "I'm proud of you" about things with no rank: asking for help, being honest, being his daughter.

Her mother learned protection wasn't control. Monitoring meant engagement. Sometimes the most powerful thing: "I don't know what you're going through, but I'm here."

The house had become what Dr. Mehra called it a "fortress of resilience" where falling didn't mean exile, where honesty was rewarded with presence.

Priya spoke at three more schools. Always ended: "You don't need to be broken to deserve help. If your home doesn't feel safe, build a different fortress: one person, one counselor, one helpline. But don't survive alone. Don't let silence kill you."

A boy approached after, voice low: "What if you've already started?"

She recognized his eyes. Had worn them herself.

"Tell one person today. Not tomorrow. Today." She wrote down Dr. Mehra's number, NMBA helpline. "They answer. They don't judge. They help you find the way back."

"Back to what?"

"To yourself. To the version that doesn't need an escape route from your own life."

He took the paper. I folded it carefully. A promise.

Driving home, Priya asked: "Would it have been different if we'd talked earlier?"

Her mother considered it. "Maybe. But we can't go back. Only build forward."

"How do you build a fortress?"

"One honest conversation at a time. One dinner where everyone shows up. One moment where you choose truth over performance." She glanced at Priya. "It's not dramatic. Just consistently ordinary."

The kind of ordinary that saves lives.

At dinner, her father asked: "What was something real today?"

Priya answered: "A kid asked for help. And I had something to give him."

Her father smiled. Not about rank or achievement. Just pride in who she was becoming messy, recovering, real.

"That's my girl," he said.

And for the first time in years, Priya believed him.

What you can do next >>>

For Students	For Parents	For Teachers
Practice Refusal: Rehearse specific ways to say "no" to peer pressure without "losing face".	**Ritualize Connection:** Implement simple family rituals, like phone-free dinners, to build emotional safety and bonding.	**Integrate Life Skills:** Move beyond "shock and awe" lectures; teach mindfulness and critical media literacy in regular lessons.
Find a "3 AM Person": Identify one trusted adult you can call if you ever feel the pull to experiment or are in trouble.	**Warm Monitoring:** Show an active interest in your child's friends and digital life without making it feel like "surveillance".	**Compassionate Referral:** If a student is caught using, prioritize a referral to the NMBA helpline (14446) over immediate expulsion.

CHAPTER 3

The Adolescent Brain and Addiction

3.1 The Biological Imperative of Vulnerability

To combat the epidemic, one must understand the biology of vulnerability. The brain of an adolescent (roughly 12–25 years) is structurally and functionally different from an adult's, making it uniquely susceptible to developing dependence.

The developing brain matures from back to front:

- **Limbic System (Emotional Center):** This area, responsible for immediate pleasure, reward, and emotion, matures early. It is hyper-responsive to the dopamine rush induced by substances.
- **Prefrontal Cortex (PFC):** This area, responsible for "executive functions" like judgment, impulse control, risk assessment, and long-term planning, is the last to fully develop (often not until the mid-twenties).

The result is a period of **maximum risk**: a fully operational emotional engine (Limbic System) driving impulsive seeking behavior, combined with an underdeveloped braking mechanism (PFC). Substances effectively hijack the pleasure circuit, teaching the young brain to prioritize immediate gratification over long-term consequences.

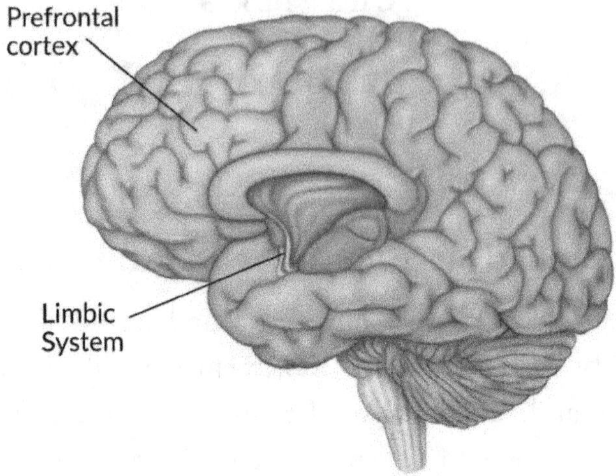

3.2 The Gateway Theory and Early Initiation

The age of first use is a critical predictive factor for lifetime addiction severity. The mean age of initiation into drug abuse in India is approximately 24 years, but 9.7% of users start before the age of 15, and an additional 25-30% begin between 16 and 20 years of age.

Early use often follows a **Gateway Pattern**:

1. **Phase I:** Legal substances (Tobacco, Alcohol).
2. **Phase II:** Cannabis and Inhalants (due to accessibility and peer acceptance).
3. **Phase III:** Harder substances (Opioids, Injectables, Cocaine).

Each step in this progression further primes the developing brain for deeper dependency. NGO reports from treatment centers show that children who begin with inhalants or tobacco at 10–12 years old are at significantly higher risk of escalating to opioid injection by their late teens, highlighting the necessity of hyper-vigilance in early adolescence.

3.3 The Comorbidity Challenge: Dual Diagnosis

A crucial finding recognized by modern psychiatry and treatment facilities is the high rate of **Comorbidity** the simultaneous presence of a mental health disorder and a Substance Use Disorder (SUD). Substance abuse is often a symptom, not the root cause.

- **Self-Medication:** Many young people use drugs or alcohol to "self-medicate" untreated anxiety, depression, social phobia, or trauma. They discover that a substance temporarily silences the pain, creating a reinforcing cycle of use.
- **The Bi-directional Link:** This relationship is bi-directional. While pre-existing mental health issues can lead to drug use, chronic drug use itself causes neurochemical changes that can induce or worsen psychiatric symptoms, including anxiety, psychosis, and severe depression.

The challenge for Integrated Rehabilitation Centres for Addicts (IRCAs) and community counselors is addressing both conditions simultaneously. Treatment must move beyond simply managing addiction withdrawal; it must incorporate psychiatric counseling, trauma therapy, and mental wellness strategies to ensure long-term sobriety. This **dual-diagnosis** approach is the benchmark for effective recovery.

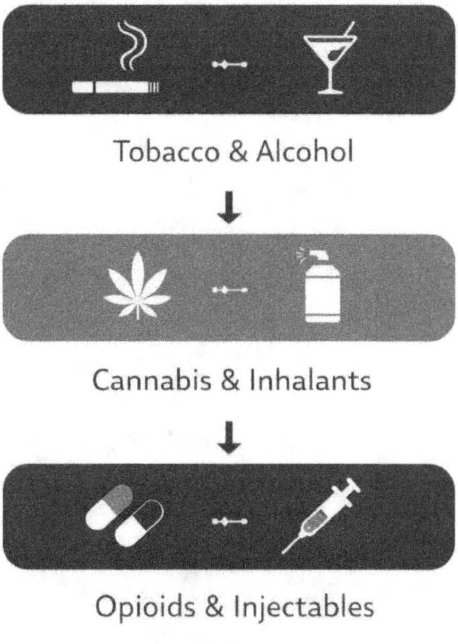

Part II

Prevention:

Building the Defense Mechanism

CHAPTER 4

The Pillars of Prevention: The Family Mandate

4.1 The Family as the First Line of Defense

Prevention is a multi-layered defense system, and the family unit forms the foundational layer. While external factors, peer pressure, availability, media are potent risk factors, the presence of **strong familial protective factors** can neutralize or significantly mitigate these threats. In the Indian context, where family ties and kinship structures are traditionally strong, leveraging this inherent support system is paramount to effective drug prevention.

The family is responsible for establishing the first set of social norms, ethical values, and coping mechanisms. When this foundation is fractured by neglect, conflict, or lack of engagement, the child's vulnerability increases dramatically. NMBA's strategy recognizes that a healed family is often the catalyst for a successful recovery journey and, more importantly, the most effective barrier against initiation.

4.2 Building Resilience : Protective Factors in the Home

Research consistently identifies three core protective factors rooted in the family environment:

a. Strong Family Bonding and Attachment

Emotional attachment provides a sense of belonging and security. When youth feel valued and loved unconditionally, they are less likely to seek emotional fulfillment or escapism in substances. This involves quality time, shared activities (even simple rituals like eating dinner together), and expressions of affection and pride.

b. Parental Monitoring and Supervision

This involves knowing where the child is, who they are with, and what they are doing. Effective monitoring is not surveillance; it is an active, warm interest in the child's life. Crucially, studies show that youth are less likely to engage in high-risk behaviors when they perceive their parents would disapprove and that this disapproval is backed by loving vigilance. This is particularly vital in the context of increased digital presence and online peer groups, requiring parents to monitor digital activity without invading privacy.

c. Clear Rules and Consistent Discipline

Substance use prevention requires clear, non-negotiable family rules regarding substance abuse. These rules must be established early and enforced consistently, but always accompanied by warmth and explanation. Disciplinary action should focus on teaching rather than punishment, reinforcing the understanding of consequences and responsibility. Inconsistency (e.g., forbidding use but using substances heavily oneself) is a major risk factor.

4.3 Fostering Non-Judgmental Communication

Perhaps the single most powerful tool in the family arsenal is open communication. A child must feel that they can approach a parent with any problem, academic failure, bullying, or even experimentation with substances, without fear of immediate punishment or shaming.

- **Active Listening:** This is more than just hearing words; it's about validating feelings. When a parent listens without interrupting, offering advice, or judging, they create a 'safe space.'

- **The "What If" Scenario:** Instead of direct confrontation, parents can use hypothetical scenarios to initiate conversation: "If someone offered you a cigarette at a party, what would you do?" This allows the youth to practice decision-making skills in a safe environment.
- **Talking about Mental Health:** Given the high comorbidity rate (Chapter 3), parents must proactively discuss stress, anxiety, and depression. Normalizing these feelings removes the incentive for self-medication and encourages seeking healthy support. Parents should be educated on how to spot the early signs of mental distress.

4.4 Empowering the Caregiver: NMBA's Role in Parental Training

The National Drug De-addiction Strategy (NDDS) and NMBA recognize that parents often lack the specific skills to address this modern crisis. A parent who effectively navigated the challenges of the 1990s may not be equipped to handle the complexities of online drug access and synthetic substances today.

NMBA focuses on **Caregiver Training Modules** delivered through NGOs and NMBA Master Volunteers. These modules should cover:

1. **Early Warning Signs:** Recognizing the subtle behavioral, physical, and psychological indicators of substance use (e.g., changes in sleep patterns, sudden secrecy, drop in grades).
2. **Intervention Scripts:** Providing parents with concrete, evidence-based language to initiate difficult conversations, avoiding accusatory tones.
3. **Stress Management for Parents:** Recognizing that parental stress and conflict are themselves risk factors. NMBA

programs should offer support systems for caregivers dealing with their own stressors.

4. **Harm Reduction and Help-Seeking:** Educating parents on the immediate steps to take if they discover substance use, primarily focusing on seeking professional help (helplines, counselors) rather than domestic disciplinary actions that can drive the user further away.

The ultimate goal of the Family Mandate is to transform the home from a potential source of stress into a **fortress of resilience**, where the child's self-esteem and critical thinking skills are nurtured to the point where external temptations become secondary to internal strength.

CHAPTER 5

School as the First Line of Defense: Evidence-Based Curricula

5.1 The School as a Controlled Environment for Social Growth

After the home, the school is the single most important institution for shaping behavior during formative years (6-18 years). Educational institutions serve as microcosms of society where youth navigate social hierarchies, manage performance anxiety, and confront peer influence. For millions of Indian children, especially those in rural and low-income areas, the school represents the only stable, formal environment where they can be exposed to consistent messaging outside of their immediate family.

A holistic school-based prevention strategy is effective because it targets risk factors (**peer pressure, academic stress**) and enhances protective factors (**self-esteem, critical thinking, connection to positive role models**) at scale. The goal is to evolve the school from a center of pure academic instruction into a **Comprehensive Wellness Centre**.

5.2 Moving Beyond Scare Tactics: The Efficacy of Life Skills Education

Decades of research have shown that prevention programs based purely on fear-mongering or dramatic presentations of negative consequences (often called **'Shock and Awe'** campaigns) are largely ineffective and can sometimes backfire, increasing curiosity. Effective prevention is based on **Social and Emotional Learning (SEL)** and must be evidence-based, focusing on practical life skills.

NMBA's approach advocates for curricula that teach:

1. **Refusal Skills and Assertiveness:** Giving students concrete, rehearsed language and strategies to decline offers of drugs or alcohol without losing face, thereby combating peer pressure effectively.
2. **Critical Media Literacy:** Training students to recognize the subtle and overt glorification of substance use in advertising, cinema, and digital media, and to critically evaluate the risks versus the perceived glamour.
3. **Stress Management and Coping Mechanisms:** Introducing techniques like mindfulness, deep breathing, and positive self-talk to deal with the intense pressure of competitive exams and family expectations, providing healthy alternatives to self-medication.

This education should not be a one-off annual lecture but a **sequential, developmentally-appropriate curriculum** integrated throughout grades 6 to 12. For instance, basic facts about inhalants and poisons for younger children (6-10) should graduate to complex decision-making and mental health links for adolescents (14-18).

5.3 Training the Gatekeepers: Empowering Teachers and Counselors

The best curriculum is ineffective if the delivery mechanism is compromised. Teachers, principals, and school counselors are the primary gatekeepers, yet they often lack the specialized training to address SUDs effectively.

- **NMBA Master Volunteer Integration:** NMBA Master Volunteers and trained NMBA-NGO personnel should conduct mandatory training workshops for all school staff (teaching and non-teaching) at least twice a year.
- **Early Identification and Referral:** Teachers must be trained to recognize the subtle, non-disruptive signs of early use (fatigue, sudden shifts in friend groups, unexplained resource consumption, e.g., money or household chemicals). The focus must be on compassionate referral to the school counselor or NMBA helpline, not immediate expulsion or public humiliation.
- **The School Counselor's Enhanced Role:** The role of the school counselor must move beyond career guidance. They need advanced training in motivational interviewing, brief intervention techniques, and maintaining strict confidentiality to establish trust with students. Their mandate is to act as the primary link between the student, the family, and external treatment centres (IRCAs).

5.4 Establishing Institutional Accountability and Policies

Prevention strategies must be backed by clear, consistent, and compassionate institutional policy. Ambiguous policies lead to arbitrary enforcement, often damaging a student's future through punitive measures rather than restorative ones.

- **Anti-Drug and Wellness Committees:** Every educational institution (secondary school and higher education) should mandate a standing committee composed of the Principal, a Counselor, a Teacher Representative, a Parent Representative, and a trained NMBA Master Volunteer. This committee is responsible for policy, outreach, and managing crisis situations.

- **Zero Tolerance, but Compassionate Treatment:** While the policy must be 'Zero Tolerance' for drug dealing or actively endangering others, a policy concerning student *use* must prioritize rehabilitation. The policy should include mandatory counseling, parental involvement, and structured reintegration plans rather than immediate, permanent exclusion, which simply pushes the vulnerable user out of the formal support system.
- **Regular Parent-Teacher Sensitization:** Just as parents receive training (Chapter 4), schools must host compulsory workshops for parents focusing on current drug trends, NMBA resources, and the importance of collaborative monitoring, bridging the gap between home and school.

5.5 Harnessing Positive Peer Influence: Student-Led Initiatives

Peer influence, often cited as a major risk factor, can be deliberately leveraged as a powerful protective factor. Peer educators are more relatable, credible, and often more effective at transmitting social norms than adult authority figures.

- **NMBA Youth Clubs:** Schools should be encouraged to establish official NMBA Youth Clubs where student leaders (aged 16+) are rigorously trained by NMBA volunteers. These students can then:
    - Organize awareness events and street plays (Nukkad Nataks) that resonate culturally.

- Disseminate factual, non-judgemental information about drug use and mental health.
- Act as positive role models, demonstrating healthy coping mechanisms for stress.

By implementing a multi-pronged approach, integrating SEL into curricula, empowering staff, and enforcing compassionate, clear policies, the school environment transforms from a place of potential risk into a **primary bastion of resilience** for India's youth.

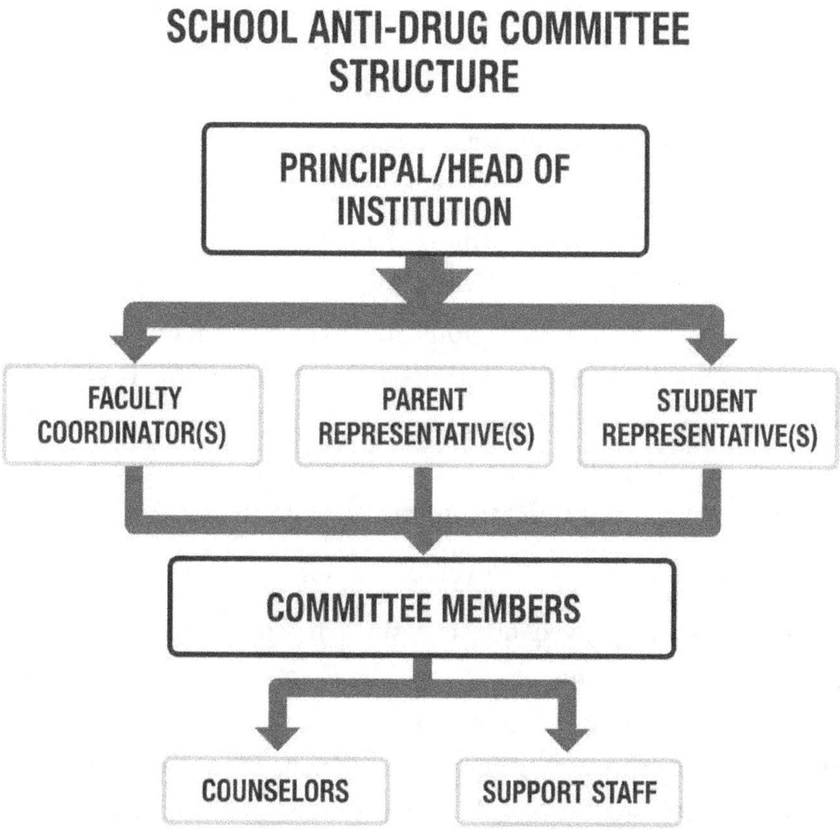

STORY 3

The Weight of a Secret

A Story of Transformation in Room 7-B

The morning assembly droned on in its predictable cadence national anthem, principal's announcements, the perfunctory dispersal. But in the third row of Class 7-B, sixteen-year-old **Aditya Malhotra** stood with his hands clenched, knuckles white against the seams of his navy-blue trousers. To the undiscerning eye, he was merely another student enduring the morning ritual. To those who knew where to look, he was a boy drowning in plain sight.

Three months prior, Aditya had been the embodiment of promise, a scholarship student whose brilliance had earned him a coveted seat at Delhi's prestigious St. Xavier's Academy. His mother, a widow who stitched garments in a cramped Karol Bagh apartment, had wept tears of vindication the day the acceptance letter arrived. Her son would transcend their circumstances. He would become something she could only dream of.

But dreams, Aditya discovered, cast long shadows.

The pressure arrived not as a sudden storm but as a relentless drizzle each coaching class, each benchmark examination, each whispered comparison to his wealthier classmates accumulating like monsoon water with nowhere to drain. Sleep became a luxury he could no longer afford. His mind, once sharp as a blade, grew dull with exhaustion. And then, on an unremarkable Tuesday, his classmate **Rohan,** charming, affluent, effortlessly brilliant Rohan, had offered him a solution wrapped in silver foil.

"Just to focus, yaar. Everyone's doing it. How do you think Sharma topped last semester?"

The first time, it had been curiosity laced with desperation. The second time, necessity. By the third, Aditya no longer needed convincing.

Mrs. Kavita Sengupta had taught English literature at St. Xavier's for seventeen years, long enough to recognize the archipelago of adolescent troubles, unrequited crushes, academic anxiety, the perennial drama of friendship betrayals. But something about Aditya troubled her in a way she couldn't immediately articulate.

It wasn't the obvious signs. He hadn't become belligerent or truant. Rather, it was the *subtraction* she noticed the gradual disappearance of the boy who once stayed after class to debate the motivations of Macbeth, who had written an essay on Partition literature so moving she'd kept a copy in her desk drawer. Now, he sat at the back, a ghost inhabiting his own body, his once-luminous eyes clouded with something she couldn't name.

The revelation came not through surveillance but through accident. Tidying the classroom after the final bell, Mrs. Sengupta discovered a crumpled note beneath Aditya's desk: *"Same place. 4 PM. Don't be late. You still owe me 500."*

Her heart performed an unwelcome somersault. She'd attended the mandatory NMBA training workshop the previous semester, one of those sessions teachers often dismissed as administrative checkbox exercises. But the trainer, a former counselor named **Mr. Vikram Khanna**, had been different. He'd spoken not in abstractions but in anatomies of real cases, teaching them to recognize the cartography of early substance use: the fatigue masquerading as laziness, the social realignment, the inexplicable need for money.

"The greatest tragedy," he'd said, his voice carrying the weight of witnessed devastation, "is not that we fail to see the signs. It's that we see them and do nothing, convinced that intervention is beyond our mandate or competence."

Mrs. Sengupta had nodded politely then, never imagining she'd be holding evidence of a student's unraveling in her trembling hands just months later.

The conversation happened not in the principal's office, a space designed for judgment but in the school counselor's room, a deliberately modest space softened by plants and natural light. **Ms. Priya Reddy**, newly trained in motivational interviewing through the NMBA's enhanced counselor program, had learned that the setting mattered almost as much as the words.

Aditya entered with the defensive posture of a cornered animal, ready for accusation and punishment. Instead, Ms. Reddy gestured to a comfortable chair and asked a disarming question: "How heavy does it feel, carrying this alone?"

The question, so unexpected in its compassion, shattered something in him. Not immediately adolescent pride is a formidable fortress but gradually, as Ms. Reddy listened without horror, without disappointment theatrical enough to weaponize his shame. She didn't ask "Why?" as if substance use were an incomprehensible moral failing. She asked "What do you need?" as if recovery were not just possible but expected.

"I just wanted to keep up," Aditya finally whispered, the confession extracted not through interrogation but through the simple radical act of being heard. "Everyone else seems to manage. I thought... I thought if I could just focus better, study harder, I could make my mother proud. I could justify her sacrifice."

"And now?" Ms. Reddy's voice remained steady, a lighthouse in his storm.

"Now I can't stop. Even when I want to."

What followed was not a fairytale transformation recovery never is. The school's Anti-Drug and Wellness Committee convened, not to expel but to construct a support infrastructure. Aditya's mother was brought in, not with recrimination but with resources. The NMBA helpline provided connection to an Integrated Rehabilitation Centre for Addicts (IRCA) offering subsidized treatment.

But perhaps the most profound intervention came from an unexpected quarter: the newly formed **NMBA Youth Club**.

Meera, a senior who'd lost her brother to addiction three years prior, had channeled her grief into prevention work. When she learned of Aditya's situation maintaining strict confidentiality about specifics she approached him not as a project but as a peer who understood that vulnerability wasn't weakness.

"You know what took me years to learn?" she said one afternoon as they organized a wellness awareness event. "That asking for help isn't failing. It's the opposite. It's refusing to let the weight crush you alone."

The Youth Club's first major initiative was a street play, a nukkad *natak*, performed during the school's annual cultural festival. Written collaboratively by students, it depicted not the lurid stereotypes of addiction but its more insidious reality: the straight-A student who starts using "study drugs," the athlete taking painkillers, the artist seeking chemical inspiration. It showed how easily anyone could stumble, and how crucial it was that the community catch them.

The performance ended not with a death scene designed to shock, but with a circle of students extending hands to a fallen peer. The symbolism was deliberate: recovery was communal, not solitary.

Eighteen months later, Aditya stood before the same morning assembly, but this time at the podium. He'd been invited to speak as part of the school's mental health awareness week not as a cautionary tale reduced to his worst moments, but as a testament to resilience.

"I won't pretend it was easy," he said, his voice steady now, strengthened by therapy, support, and the grueling work of rebuilding trust with himself and others. "There were days I wanted to give up. Days I was convinced I'd destroyed every opportunity I'd been given."

He paused, scanning the sea of faces, some attentive, some distracted, all of them carrying invisible weights he couldn't see but understood were there.

"But I learned something crucial: we've constructed this mythology that struggle means failure, that needing help means weakness, that the only acceptable path is solitary perfection. It's a lie. And it's killing us."

Mrs. Sengupta, standing at the side of the assembly hall, felt tears prick her eyes not of sorrow but of recognition. The boy who'd nearly vanished had returned, transmuted by ordeal into something both harder and more tender than before.

"The school saved my life," Aditya continued. "Not by punishing me. Not by making an example of me. But by treating me like a human being worthy of redemption. By having systems in place counselors who knew how to help, teachers who knew what to look for, peers who refused to let me disappear."

He glanced toward Ms. Reddy, toward Mrs. Sengupta, toward Meera standing with the Youth Club members, their green awareness ribbons visible against their uniforms.

"If you're struggling with substances, with pressure, with the weight of expectations please know: you don't have to carry it alone. The school isn't just a place for grades and examinations. It can be, should be, your first line of defense. Your sanctuary. Your chance to become who you're meant to be, not who fear and desperation convince you to be."

The assembly dispersed, students flowing toward their respective classrooms in the usual controlled chaos. But something subtle had shifted an invisible recalibration of the school's emotional atmosphere. Teachers who'd attended the NMBA training paid closer attention. Students in the Youth Club wore their identification badges with quiet pride. The counselor's office, once stigmatized, saw increased traffic from students seeking help before the crisis, not after.

The school had evolved, incrementally but irreversibly, from an institution focused solely on academic metrics to something more holistic: a **Comprehensive Wellness Centre** where a student's worth was measured not just by examination scores but by their wholeness, their resilience, their capacity to seek and extend help.

And in Room 7-B, where Aditya had once sat drowning in silence, a new student shy, overwhelmed, visibly struggling noticed the NMBA Youth Club poster on the wall. After class, she approached Mrs. Sengupta with a question that might once have gone unasked: "Is it really okay to ask for help?"

Mrs. Sengupta smiled, recognizing the courage that question required. "Not just okay," she said gently. "Essential. Let me tell you about some resources we have..."

The cycle continued, but this time, with intention. With infrastructure. With institutional compassion that transformed abstract policy into lived salvation.

This was prevention not as a dramatic intervention, but as a deliberate architecture of care, built brick by brick, policy by policy, conversation by conversation. The school had become what it was always meant to be: not just a crucible of academic achievement, but a sanctuary where young lives, in all their beautiful fragility, were protected, nurtured, and given the tools to flourish.

The first line of defense, holding firm.

CHAPTER 6

Empowerment Through Engagement: Leveraging Youth Potential

6.1 The Transition: From Target Group to Change Agent

The success of *Nasha Mukt Navnirman* rests on a fundamental paradigm shift: treating youth not merely as the **target group** of prevention efforts, but as the **primary agents of change**. The youth demographic possesses inherent strengths that are uniquely effective in combating substance abuse: cultural relevance, instant credibility among peers, technological fluency, and a passion for social justice.

When preventative messages are delivered by peers who understand the immediate pressures of academic life, social media, and competitive stress, the impact is dramatically higher than messages delivered solely by adult authority figures. Empowerment through engagement means providing young people with the training, platforms, and resources necessary to design, lead, and sustain the anti-drug movement at the grassroots level.

6.2 The NMBA Master Volunteer (MV) Framework: The Backbone

The NMBA Master Volunteer (MV) framework is the foundational structure for organized youth mobilization. These are young leaders (often college students or recent graduates) who undergo intensive, standardized training to become resource persons in their communities.

a. Rigorous, Standardized Training

MV training must transcend mere awareness and focus on **skill-building**. Key components include:

1. **Motivational Interviewing (MI) Basics:** Training in non-confrontational communication techniques essential for sensitive conversations with those considering or struggling with substance use.
2. **Crisis Triage and Referral Pathways:** Understanding local NMBA partner NGOs, IRCAs, and the NMBA helpline (14446), ensuring they can provide immediate, actionable next steps rather than just advice.
3. **Data Collection and Reporting:** Training MVs to use digital tools (mobile apps) for systematic, ethical data collection on local drug availability and high-risk pockets, enabling evidence-based policymaking at the district level.

b. Credibility and Cultural Proximity

The MV, often residing in the same community or attending the same university, shares a cultural and linguistic context with the at-risk population. This proximity allows for the creation of preventative content that is immediately relatable and avoids the patronizing tone often associated with government messaging.

6.3 Harnessing the Digital and Creative Ecosystem

The drug crisis today is deeply interwoven with the digital landscape, where substances are glamorized, advertised, and even procured. Youth engagement must meet the epidemic where it lives, online.

a. Digital Advocacy: Countering the Narrative

Young volunteers are best positioned to combat the online normalization of drug use through **counter-narratives.** This involves:

- **Fact-Checking and Debunking:** Creating short, engaging videos (micro-content) that scientifically debunk myths and misinformation prevalent on platforms like WhatsApp and Instagram regarding drug effects and safety.
- **The Power of Personal Testimony:** Sharing compelling, anonymous stories of recovery and resilience (vetted by counselors) to demonstrate that the path to addiction is real, but so is the path to recovery.
- **Ethical Influencing:** Training youth to use their social media reach not for celebrity endorsement, but for genuine, positive influence, promoting mental health coping mechanisms and NMBA resources.

b. Cultural and Artistic Mobilization (Nukkad Nataks and Beyond)

Traditional Indian cultural forms are powerful tools for localized engagement, especially in rural and semi-urban settings.

- **Nukkad Nataks (Street Plays):** NMBA-sponsored youth theatre groups should stage street plays that dramatize common local triggers (e.g., family conflict, academic pressure, peer bullying) and offer clear, culturally appropriate solutions.
- **Rap and Regional Music:** Youth should be encouraged to write and perform music in local languages that addresses the drug crisis, using contemporary rhythms to deliver positive, hard-hitting messages about empowerment and sobriety.

6.4 Structured Opportunities for Sustained Engagement

To maintain long-term commitment, youth engagement cannot be a sporadic activity; it must offer tangible benefits that contribute to their personal and professional development (the "What's In It For Me" factor).

a. Skill-Building and Certification

Participation must offer accredited skill enhancement. NMBA could partner with vocational institutes to provide certifications to MVs in areas directly applicable to their service:

Service Skill	Certifiable Competency	Career Relevance
Counseling/ Referral	Applied Crisis Intervention (NMBA Level I)	Social Work, Psychology, Healthcare
Data Collection	Digital Survey and Field Research Methods	Public Policy, Market Research
Outreach/ Advocacy	Public Speaking and Persuasive Communication	Management, Law, Civil Services

b. Mentorship and Career Pathway

Active NMBA youth should be linked with established professionals (doctors, police officers, civil servants, entrepreneurs) who can provide mentorship. This connects the abstract idea of a "drug-free future" with a concrete career pathway, demonstrating that their commitment today opens doors tomorrow. The mentor-mentee relationship reinforces positive social norms and provides an alternative source of validation outside of peer groups.

6.5 Conclusion: The Multiplier Effect of Agency

Empowerment through engagement is the ultimate protective factor. When a young person actively chooses to become a solution-provider, they develop a profound sense of self-efficacy and purpose. This internalized commitment not only shields them from personal vulnerability but creates a **multiplier effect** in their social circles, transforming communities one motivated leader at a time. The NMBA's true success is measured not just by the number of campaigns conducted, but by the number of young Indians who transform from potential victims into determined, highly-skilled victors.

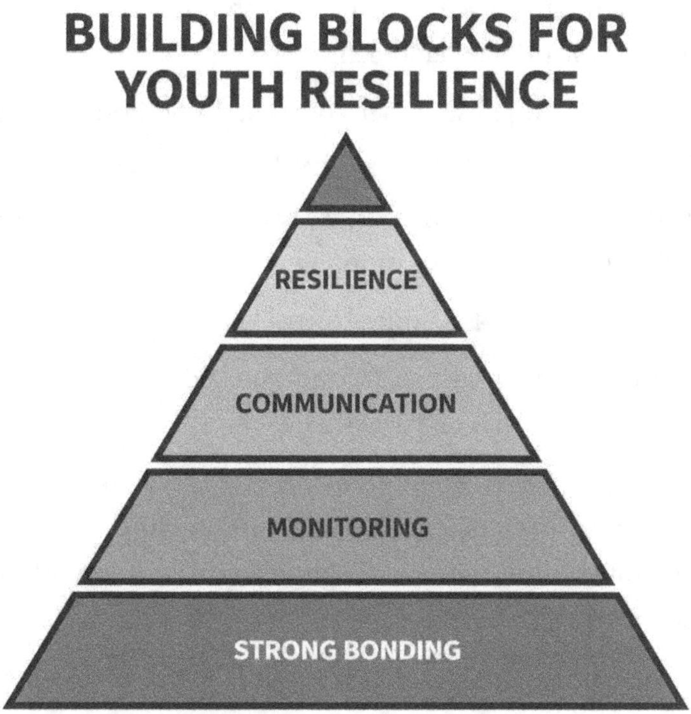

STORY 4

The Distance Between Us

A Story of Reconnection Across the Kitchen Table

The clock on the kitchen wall read 11:47 PM when **Anjali Sharma** finally heard the front door click open. She didn't move from her position at the dining table, hands wrapped around a cup of tea that had long gone cold. Her husband, **Rajesh**, sat across from her, his newspaper unread, folded into precise thirds, a prop for hands that didn't know what else to hold.

Their daughter **Naina** entered with the practiced stealth of someone who'd perfected the art of invisibility. Sixteen years old, a scholarship student at one of Mumbai's premier colleges, their pride incarnate or at least, she had been.

"You're late," Anjali said, her voice carefully modulated to avoid the accusation that crouched behind every syllable.

"Coaching ran over." Naina's response came automatically, rehearsed. She didn't see her mother's eyes.

"Your coaching ends at nine-thirty."

A pause, pregnant with everything unsaid. Then: "Group study session. We have prelims next week."

It was a lie. Anjali knew it was a lie. The recognition sat like broken glass in her chest, sharp and unforgiving. When did her brilliant, honest, transparent daughter become someone who lied with such fluency?

Naina disappeared into her room, the door closing with a softness that felt somehow worse than a slam. At least anger was honest.

"She's just stressed," Rajesh offered weakly, the same words he'd been offering for three months now, as if repetition might transform them into truth. "Board exams, entrance coaching, the pressure we never had to face "

"Rajesh." Anjali's voice cracked like a whip. "When did we become the kind of parents who see the fire but convince ourselves it's just the light?"

Six months earlier, Naina had been incandescent with purpose. She'd secured admission to a prestigious junior college on full scholarship, the first in their middle-class Borivali household to achieve such distinction. Rajesh, who managed a small textile business, had hosted a celebration dinner, inviting relatives who'd once looked down on their modest circumstances. Anjali had watched her daughter glow under the attention, already imagining the future: medical school, perhaps, or engineering. Something prestigious. Something worthy of the sacrifice.

The scholarship covered tuition, but the hidden costs of coaching classes for competitive exams, study materials, and the social expectations of studying alongside Mumbai's elite had proven more insidious. While Naina's classmates arrived in chauffeur-driven cars, designer backpacks slung casually over shoulders, she took two buses, her materials photocopied, her clothes carefully preserved.

She never complained. That was the tragedy Anjali would later recognize Naina had never once articulated the chasm between her world and theirs, between aspiration and resource, between what was expected and what was possible.

The changes had been glacial, easy to misinterpret. Naina withdrew into her room, which seemed natural for a student facing academic rigor. She became irritable, which they attributed to adolescence and stress. Her appetite diminished, her sleep patterns erratic, all explainable within the framework of competitive examination culture that consumed Indian teenagers like a benevolent monster.

But then came the morning Anjali found **₹5,000 missing** from the household emergency fund she kept in the steel cupboard. When confronted, Naina had stammered something about needing to pay coaching fees in advance, a story that didn't quite cohere but which Rajesh had accepted with relief. Questions were dangerous; they might reveal answers they weren't prepared to confront.

The second incident was harder to dismiss. Anjali's gold earrings, not expensive but sentimental, a wedding gift from her late mother vanished from the dressing table. Naina claimed ignorance, suggesting perhaps the maid had taken them. The accusation, so uncharacteristic of her daughter's usual compassion, had sent ice through Anjali's veins.

Something was catastrophically wrong. She simply hadn't wanted to name it.

The revelation came not through parental investigation but through unwitting confession. Anjali returned home early from her part-time teaching job one afternoon, unwell with a migraine that made her skull feel fragile as eggshell. She found Naina in the bathroom, hunched over the sink with something in her hands.

Their eyes met in the mirror. Naina's face cycled through expressions in rapid succession shock, defiance, resignation, and finally, something that looked almost like relief. The relief of someone who'd been drowning and had finally stopped fighting the current.

"Mumma," she whispered, and the word contained such devastation that Anjali felt her knees weaken.

What followed was not a confrontation but a collapse. Naina sank to the bathroom floor, and for the first time in months, she told the truth. About **Shreya**, her classmate who'd introduced her to pills that promised focus and stamina. About how everyone seemed to be using caffeine pills at minimum, prescription stimulants for the serious students, and for those who couldn't afford prescriptions, cheaper alternatives purchased from the medical store near college with fabricated excuses.

"I just wanted to keep up," Naina sobbed, her composure so carefully maintained, finally shattering. "Do you know what it's like? Sitting in a class where everyone's already three chapters ahead because they have private tutors? Where do they discuss summer programs in Singapore while I'm calculating bus fare? I thought if I could just concentrate better, study longer, I could compete. I could make you proud."

"Beta..." Anjali's voice broke on endearment. She wanted to say something profound, something healing, but all she could manage was: "How did we not see?"

That evening, when Rajesh returned from work, he found his wife and daughter sitting together on the living room sofa, tissues scattered around them like the aftermath of emotional warfare. Anjali's explanation was clinical, each word carefully selected to prevent her voice from fracturing: their daughter needed help. Professional help. Immediately.

Rajesh's first instinct was denial dressed as pragmatism. "Let's not overreact. Many students take these things. It's not like she's... it's not an addiction. She's just studying too hard."

"Rajesh." Anjali's voice carried a steel he'd rarely heard. "Our daughter stole from us to buy drugs. She lied to us for months. She's losing weight, losing sleep, losing *herself*. At what point does your pride allow you to call this what it is?"

The word hung in the air like smoke: *drugs*. Not "study aids." Not "supplements." Not the comfortable euphemisms that allowed parents to look away.

Naina watched her parents, her body curled into itself, waiting for judgment. What she received instead was something she hadn't anticipated: her father's careful lowering of himself beside her, his arm tentative, uncertain wrapping around her shoulders.

"I'm sorry," he said, and the apology carried the weight of all his absences, all the questions he'd been too afraid to ask, all the signs he'd willfully misinterpreted. "I'm sorry we made you feel you had to be perfect. That you had to sacrifice your wellbeing to meet expectations we never should have placed on you."

The next morning, Anjali made a phone call she'd been dreading. Her colleague, **Mrs. Deshmukh had** mentioned attending an **NMBA parent workshop** the previous semester, one of those government initiatives that sounded bureaucratic and abstract. But Mrs. Deshmukh had spoken about it with unusual conviction, calling it "revelatory."

The woman who answered the NMBA helpline didn't sound clinical or judgmental. Her name was **Shalini**, and she listened with the kind of attention that felt like a physical presence. She didn't gasp when Anjali described the situation. She didn't lecture about parental failure. Instead, she asked practical questions: What was Naina using? How long? What support systems did they have?

"Mrs. Sharma," Shalini said gently, "what you're experiencing is far more common than you imagine. The shame makes parents suffer in isolation, convinced they're alone. You're not. And more importantly, there are resources specifically designed for this."

She outlined a plan: immediate consultation at an **Integrated Rehabilitation Centre for Addicts (IRCA)** that specialized in adolescent cases. A family counseling program to address underlying dynamics. Connection with a parent support group where Anjali and Rajesh could meet others navigating similar terrain.

"The most important thing," Shalini emphasized, "is that you've recognized the problem and you're seeking help. Many parents don't. They punish instead of supporting. They isolate instead of connecting. The fact that you're calling means Naina has something many struggling teenagers don't: parents who are willing to fight *for* her, not against her."

The **IRCA consultation** was held in a facility that deliberately avoided institutional coldness. The counselor, **Dr. Mehta**, was a woman in her fifties with kind eyes and zero tolerance for parental self-flagellation.

"I don't need you to perform guilt," she said during their first session, all three Sharmas present. "Guilt is useless. What I need is your commitment to understanding and change."

She explained what Anjali and Rajesh had been too afraid to research: that their daughter's substance use wasn't moral failure but a maladaptive coping mechanism for unbearable pressure. That recovery would require not just Naina's effort but systemic family transformation.

"You cannot just fix the child and return them to a dysfunctional system," Dr. Mehta said bluntly. "If the pressure remains identical, if the expectations stay unrealistic, if communication patterns don't shift, relapse becomes almost inevitable."

She assigned homework that felt almost absurd in its simplicity: **family dinners** without phones or television. **Thirty minutes daily** where each person shared one thing from their day without judgment or problem-solving. Permission for Naina to articulate needs without fear of disappointing them.

"Rebuild connection before you rebuild anything else," Dr. Mehta instructed. "She needs to know that your love isn't conditional on her performance."

The transformation was neither linear nor cinematic. There were setbacks, moments when Naina relapsed into old patterns, when Rajesh reverted to discussing examination scores, when Anjali caught herself equating achievement with worth. But slowly, painfully, they learned a new language.

They attended the **NMBA parent workshop** together on a Saturday spent in a community hall with thirty other parents, all carrying similar burdens of realization. The facilitator, a recovered addict turned counselor, spoke with brutal honesty about how families often unknowingly create environments where substance use becomes a logical escape.

"You want to know what protects children?" he asked the room. "It's not constant surveillance. It's not academic pressure that leaves no room for humanity. It's a connection. It's knowing they can fail and still be loved. It's demonstrating that their worth is intrinsic, not earned through report cards."

Anjali watched parents nod, some weeping quietly. They'd all internalized the same toxic mythology: that love meant pushing, that support meant never accepting anything less than exceptional, that their children's achievements validated their own sacrifices.

During the breakout session, she met **Kavita**, another mother whose son had struggled with addiction. They exchanged phone numbers, creating an informal support network, a reminder that they weren't alone in this particular wilderness.

Four months into recovery, Naina came to her parents with a request that required immense courage: she wanted to take a year off. Not to give up, but to reset. To receive proper treatment, to rebuild her relationship with learning, to rediscover who she was beyond examination scores.

Rajesh's first instinct was panic. A gap year meant falling behind, meant questioning from relatives, meant uncertainty. But he looked at his daughter still fragile, still healing and made a choice that contradicted everything his generation had been taught about success.

"Okay," he said simply. "What do you need from us?"

The relief on Naina's face was enough.

They structured the year around healing, not achievement. Naina continued counseling, both individual and family sessions. She joined the **NMBA Youth Club** at a nearby community center, where she met other young people in recovery. She volunteered at an NGO teaching underprivileged children, which paradoxically reminded her of her own privileges while reducing the weight of expectations.

Slowly, the girl they'd feared they'd lost began to reemerge but different. Quieter perhaps, but more authentic. Less concerned with performing perfection, more willing to exist as imperfect and human.

Eighteen months after that bathroom confrontation, Anjali sat at the same kitchen table where this story began. But this time, Naina sat across from her voluntarily, textbooks spread between them. She'd decided to resume studies, but on her own terms, enrolling in a less prestigious but less pressurized institution, choosing subjects she loved rather than those that promised lucrative careers.

"Mumma," Naina said, looking up from her biology notes, "I'm writing an essay for the college magazine. About my experience. About what happens when we prioritize performance over wellbeing."

Anjali felt something catch in her throat. "Are you sure? People will know"

"I want them to know." Naina's voice was steady. "If my story helps even one student feel less alone, or helps one parent recognize the signs earlier than you did, then maybe everything I went through has purpose beyond just my personal suffering."

Rajesh, preparing tea at the kitchen counter, turned to face them. "I'm proud of you, beta. Not because of your grades or your college or your future career. I'm proud of your courage. Of who you're choosing to become."

It was, Anjali realized, the first time he'd expressed pride unconnected to achievement. And in Naina's smile, tentative but genuine, she saw the profound relief of a child who'd finally learned she was loved not for what she accomplished, but for simply existing.

The essay, when published, created ripples beyond what Naina anticipated. Parents reached out some grateful, some defensive, all of them grappling with their own fear and recognition. The college counselor invited Naina to speak at a parent-student workshop, where she stood before an auditorium and spoke a truth that resonated like a bell:

"My parents didn't fail me by missing the signs immediately. They succeeded by what they did after: they listened. They sought help. They chose connection over punishment, healing over blame. They proved that love doesn't mean never making mistakes, it means being willing to acknowledge them and change."

In the audience, Anjali and Rajesh sat hand in hand, their own journey visible in every word their daughter spoke. They'd learned what the NMBA workshops had emphasized: that parents weren't expected to be therapists or addiction specialists. They were simply called to be present, to be willing to seek help, to create homes where honesty was possible and struggle wasn't shameful.

The family that had nearly fractured under the weight of unspoken expectations had been reforged, not into perfection, but into something more resilient: **authenticity**.

That night, after the workshop, the three of them sat in their modest living room. No television. No phones. Just tea and conversation and the revolutionary act of being together without agenda.

"Do you remember," Naina said softly, "when I was little, and we used to have those Sunday afternoons where we'd just talk? About anything and everything?"

Anjali nodded, remembering. "Before life got so busy. Before we became so focused on securing your future that we forgot about your present."

"I want that back," Naina said. "Not every day, we all have responsibilities. But sometimes. Regular times when we're just a family, not a production unit optimizing for success."

"Sundays," Rajesh declared suddenly, with the decisiveness he usually reserved for business decisions. "Every Sunday, 4 to 6 PM. Non-negotiable family time. No exam talk. No career discussions. Just us."

It was such a small commitment, yet it represented a seismic shift, from achievement as the organizing principle of family life to connection as the foundation from which everything else could grow.

And so they rebuilt, not the family they'd been, but the family they needed to become. One conversation at a time. One Sunday at a time. One moment of honest vulnerability at a time.

The distance between them, once a chasm of misunderstanding, pressure, and fear,slowly transformed into a bridge built from the materials of their shared struggle: **humility, compassion, and the courage to change**.

This was prevention, Anjali would later realize, not as protection from harm but as preparation for it. As building families resilient enough to face crisis without fracturing, honest enough to name problems without shame, and connected enough that no child ever felt they had to face their demons alone.

The first line of defense wasn't the school or the institution or the government program. It was **home**, transformed from a place of expectation into a sanctuary of belonging, where a child's worth was never conditional, and where asking for help wasn't weakness but wisdom.

The kitchen light burned late into the night, illuminating three people who'd found their way back to each other through the darkness. Imperfect, still healing, but finally, blessedly, **together**.

What you can do next >>>

For Students	For Parents	For Teachers
Become a Change Agent: Join an NMBA Youth Club or train as a Master Volunteer (MV) to lead peer-led awareness.	Seek Expert Help Early: If you suspect drug use, call the NMBA Helpline (14446) for anonymous, non-judgmental guidance.	Form a Wellness Committee: Ensure your school has a standing committee with parents and NMBA volunteers to manage crises.
Counter the Narrative: Use your digital fluency to debunk "cool" drug myths on social media.	Focus on "Recovery-First": Understand legal protections like Section 64A, which grants immunity to users who volunteer for treatment.	Support Reintegration: Help students returning from rehab with a structured plan to manage academic pressure and social stigma.

Part III

Intervention and Rehabilitation

(The Path to Recovery)

CHAPTER 7

The National Strategy in Action (NMBA): Goals and Milestones

7.1 The Genesis and Scope of NMBA

The **Nasha Mukt Bharat Abhiyaan (NMBA)**, launched by the Ministry of Social Justice and Empowerment (MoSJE), is the flagship national campaign designed to address the substance abuse crisis through a holistic, multi-pronged approach. Recognizing that addiction is a public health issue rather than a purely criminal one, the NMBA strategy shifts focus from punitive measures to prevention, treatment, and social reintegration.

The Abhiyaan's core mandate is to create a fully connected ecosystem that links vulnerable populations with support resources, government schemes, and sustained community action. Initially focused on **272 vulnerable districts** (identified based on the 2019 National Survey on the Extent and Pattern of Substance Use), the strategy is designed for phased expansion and saturation across the entire nation, moving the fight against drugs into the public consciousness.

7.2 The Three Pillars of the National Strategy

The NMBA is structured around three interconnected strategic pillars, ensuring that efforts are comprehensive, targeting different stages of the addiction cycle:

Pillar 1: Outreach and Awareness Generation

This is the campaign's most visible component, aimed at reducing stigma and disseminating factual information.

- **Mass Mobilization:** Utilizing the **Master Volunteer (MV) framework** (detailed in Chapter 6), NMBA achieves critical mass engagement through pledges, rallies, and community meetings. The goal is to make the discussion of substance abuse a public, normalized health topic, rather than a hidden shame.
- **Targeted Messaging:** Focusing awareness campaigns on high-risk populations, including youth in educational institutions, women, and high-prevalence areas like border districts and urban slums, using culturally relevant mediums like folk art, Nukkad Nataks, and regional language content.

Pillar 2: Focus on Treatment and Rehabilitation

This pillar ensures that individuals already struggling with substance use have access to immediate, dignified, and sustained clinical care.

- **Integrated Rehabilitation Centres for Addicts (IRCAs):** NMBA provides standardized support to a network of IRCAs run by NGOs. The focus is on improving the quality of care, adherence to clinical protocols, and ensuring dual-diagnosis capabilities (treating both addiction and co-occurring mental health issues).
- **De-addiction Facilities:** Enhancing the capacity of government-run hospitals and establishing dedicated Drug De-addiction Centres (DDCs) to provide detox services and medication-assisted treatment (MAT).

Pillar 3: Institutional Strengthening and Capacity Building

This pillar is dedicated to improving the human and structural resources required to manage the long-term crisis.

- **Training and Certification:** Providing specialized training for NMBA Master Volunteers, police personnel, social workers, and medical professionals in evidence-based practices like Motivational Enhancement Therapy (MET) and relapse prevention techniques.
- **Collaboration:** Forging strong partnerships with government departments (Health, Education, Home Affairs), statutory bodies (NCB, Excise), and key youth mobilization organizations (NYKS, NSS).

7.3 Key Milestones and Metrics of Success

The NMBA's accountability is measured by several quantitative and qualitative milestones, emphasizing impact over mere activity:

Milestone Area	Key Metric of Success	Strategic Goal
Community Saturation	**Master Volunteer Mobilization and Pledges:** Tracking the number of MVs trained and the volume of community members who take the 'Nasha Mukt' pledge (using digital tracking apps).	Establishing a visible, sustained grassroots presence in high-risk districts.

Milestone Area	Key Metric of Success	Strategic Goal
Outreach and Screening	**Number of People Screened and Counselled:** Tracking the utilization rate of Outreach and Drop-in Centres (ODICs) and NMBA-partnered NGOs.	Early identification and successful navigation of at-risk individuals to formal help.
Treatment Infrastructure	**IRCA Quality and Capacity:** Measuring the increase in beds available in NMBA-supported IRCAs and compliance with standardized care guidelines.	Ensuring immediate access to quality treatment without long waiting periods.
Educational Integration	**School/College Wellness Clubs Established:** Tracking the institutionalization of anti-drug and life skills education programs in high-risk educational zones.	Building generational resilience through formal, evidence-based curricula.

7.4 NMBA as the "Right Pathway"

For a young person seeking help, the NMBA is designed to be the single, integrated **pathway** that provides a seamless transition from crisis to recovery. It addresses the key barriers to seeking help:

1. **Stigma and Confidentiality:** The helpline (14446) and the non-judgmental approach of MVs ensure anonymity and confidentiality, lowering the psychological barrier to seeking help.

2. **Accessibility and Cost:** NMBA focuses on making treatment accessible geographically through ODICs and IRCAs and affordable (often free) through government grants to NGOs, addressing the financial barrier.
3. **Sustained Support:** By connecting individuals from detoxification (DDC/IRCA) to counseling (ODIC) to social reintegration (MV mentorship), the pathway provides a continuum of care essential for preventing relapse.

Ultimately, the NMBA represents the government's commitment to prioritizing the health and future of its youth. It is a social investment, recognizing that every young person steered onto the right pathway of recovery represents not just a life saved, but a productive citizen restored to the national workforce.

CHAPTER 8

Counseling, De-addiction, and Aftercare: The Recovery Process

8.1 Recovery: A Journey, Not an Event

The most profound realization in substance use treatment is that **addiction is a chronic disease**, and **recovery is a lifelong process**. A single period of detoxification, however challenging, is merely the first step. The true measure of success lies in sustained sobriety, improved quality of life, and full social reintegration. For young people, recovery often involves re-learning how to manage stress, navigate social situations, and develop a healthy identity, all without relying on substances.

The recovery process is structured into three essential stages, each with distinct goals and clinical requirements. Through the NMBA framework, this journey is designed to be **continuous and holistic**, ensuring the individual never feels abandoned once the initial crisis is over.

8.2 Stage 1: Stabilization and Detoxification (Detox)

Detoxification is the process of safely managing the acute physical withdrawal symptoms when a person stops using substances. This stage focuses entirely on medical stabilization.

a. The Role of Drug De-addiction Centres (DDCs)

DDCs, often attached to government hospitals or large Integrated Rehabilitation Centres for Addicts (IRCAs), are crucial during this phase. Detox must be conducted under medical supervision because withdrawal from certain substances (like alcohol and sedatives) can be life-threatening, and withdrawal from opioids is intensely painful and distressing.

b. Medically Assisted Treatment (MAT)

MAT is a clinically proven method that combines behavioral counseling with medications to treat substance use disorders. For young opioid users, for example, NMBA-supported DDCs often employ medications such as Buprenorphine or Naltrexone. These medicines help to:

1. **Suppress Withdrawal Symptoms:** Making the detox process tolerable and humane.
2. **Reduce Cravings:** Stabilizing brain chemistry and reducing the overwhelming urge to use.

It must be strongly emphasized that medication in this context is **treatment**, not substitution. It provides the necessary physiological stability to allow the individual to then engage meaningfully in the next, most crucial phase: therapy.

8.3 Stage 2: Core Rehabilitation (Psycho-Social Therapy)

Once physically stabilized, the individual transitions to the core phase of recovery, typically managed within an **IRCA**. The goal here is to address the underlying psychological, emotional, and social factors that led to substance use. This phase is intense, typically involving a residential stay of several weeks to months, providing a safe, drug-free environment for deep self-reflection.

a. Cognitive Behavioral Therapy (CBT)

CBT is the cornerstone of behavioral intervention. It teaches the recovering individual to identify the links between their thoughts, feelings, and actions. For a young student, this might involve:

- **Identifying Triggers:** Recognizing specific situations (e.g., academic exam stress, a particular social circle, or a specific time of day) that lead to a craving.
- **Challenging Distorted Thinking:** Replacing self-defeating thoughts ("I can't cope without drugs") with realistic, positive self-talk.
- **Developing Coping Skills:** Practicing healthy, non-substance-related ways to manage anxiety or emotional pain.

b. Motivational Enhancement Therapy (MET)

MET is particularly effective for young adults who may be ambivalent about long-term sobriety. It is a non-confrontational, patient-centered approach designed to elicit and strengthen the individual's intrinsic motivation for change. NMBA Master Volunteers and counselors are trained to use this technique to empower the youth to find *their own* reasons for recovery, moving away from external pressure.

c. Addressing Comorbidity (Dual Diagnosis)

As noted in Chapter 3, many young users suffer from co-occurring mental health disorders (like depression or anxiety). The NMBA mandates that all partner IRCAs provide **Dual-Diagnosis Treatment.** This means:

- The primary addiction and the mental health disorder are treated simultaneously by an integrated team (psychiatrist and counselor).

- Ignoring one condition severely jeopardizes the stability of the other, making integrated care non-negotiable for holistic recovery.

d. The Power of Peer and Group Therapy

In an IRCA setting, **Group Therapy** is essential. It dismantles the isolation and shame associated with addiction by allowing individuals to share experiences, build sober peer support networks, and practice new social skills in a safe environment. This peer connection begins to replace the drug-using social networks that often facilitate relapse.

8.4 Stage 3: Aftercare and Social Reintegration

The period immediately following an IRCA stay, often referred to as **Aftercare**, is the most fragile and the highest risk period for relapse. Aftercare is the long-term support system required to navigate the return to everyday life (family, college, work) without the protective bubble of the residential centre.

a. Relapse Prevention Planning (RPP)

RPP is a personalized strategy developed with the counselor, covering:

- **Trigger Avoidance:** Practical steps to change routines, friends, and environments that might trigger a craving.
- **Emergency Contact List:** Immediate access to the NMBA Helpline (14446), sponsor, MV, or counselor in a moment of crisis.
- **Lifestyle Balance:** Structured plans for diet, exercise, and leisure activities that fill the emotional and time void left by drug use.

b. The Critical Role of Family Therapy

Since the family is the first defense (Chapter 4), their involvement in aftercare is non-negotiable. **Family Therapy** helps to:

- Heal the trust fractured by addiction.
- Educate family members on how to support, rather than enable, recovery.
- Re-establish healthy boundaries and communication patterns (the **Non-Judgmental Communication** discussed earlier).

c. Vocational and Educational Restoration

Restoring dignity and future prospects is a powerful driver of long-term recovery. NMBA partners often work to link recovering youth with government schemes or NGO programs that provide **vocational Training** (e.g., IT skills, trades) or support their re-entry into education. A young person with a tangible, positive future goal is far less likely to be pulled back by the shadows of the past.

d. Sustained Community Support

This phase relies heavily on the **NMBA Master Volunteer (MV) mentorship** and community-based support groups (like Narcotics Anonymous or groups adapted locally). The MV acts as a sober guide and mentor, reinforcing the positive choices made in treatment and helping the young person reintegrate into a healthy peer network, cementing their status as a **determined, highly-skilled victor**.

NATIONAL DRUG STRATEGY: A ROADMAP TO RECOVERY

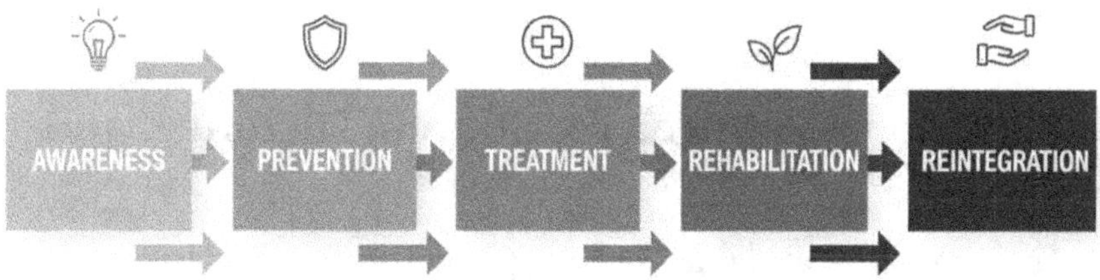

Towards a Healthier, Drug-Free Nation

CHAPTER 9

The Role of Technology and Helplines: Accessibility in Treatment

9.1 Overcoming Barriers: Stigma, Distance, and Anonymity

The two most formidable barriers preventing young Indians from accessing substance abuse treatment are **stigma** and **geographical distance**. Addiction remains heavily moralized in Indian society, leading to intense shame and secrecy. Simultaneously, specialized treatment centers (IRCAs and DDCs) are concentrated in urban clusters, leaving vast rural and semi-urban populations without immediate help.

Technology is the critical enabler for the NMBA to bridge this gap. By leveraging the ubiquity of mobile phones and the growing digital footprint of the youth, NMBA transforms inaccessible, stigmatized care into confidential, immediate, and scalable support. The NMBA's technological strategy is defined by two primary objectives: **democratizing access** and **maintaining anonymity**.

9.2 The Lifeline: The National Toll-Free Helpline (14446)

The NMBA National Helpline, *Nasha Mukt Bharat Abhiyaan Ki Sahayata Rekha* (14446), is the single most important intervention tool. It functions as the central nervous system of the entire NMBA network, providing a human connection 24 hours a day in multiple regional languages.

a. Immediate Crisis Intervention and Triage

The primary function of the helpline is not long-term counseling, but **crisis intervention and immediate triage**. Counselors are trained to:

1. **Assess Severity:** Rapidly evaluate the caller's risk level, addressing immediate threats of overdose, self-harm, or severe withdrawal symptoms.
2. **Provide Psychoeducation:** Offer immediate, practical advice on managing acute cravings or dealing with a crisis situation.
3. **Warm Hand-off:** This is the most critical step. The helpline is responsible for connecting the caller (or the family member calling on their behalf) to the closest, most appropriate resource, be it a DDC for medical detox, an IRCA for residential care, an NGO-run Outreach and Drop-In Centre (ODIC), or a local NMBA Master Volunteer (MV).

b. Anonymity as the Primary Enabler

The non-threatening nature of a phone call, where identity is not immediately demanded, encourages high-risk youth, who might never walk into a physical center, to take the first step. The helpline is the **confidential conduit** through which hidden distress can be surfaced and addressed. Data collected from helpline usage provides real-time, invaluable insights into current substance trends and geographical hotspots, which often precede formal survey data.

9.3 Digital Tools for Master Volunteers and Outreach

The Master Volunteer (MV) network, the human face of NMBA on the ground (Chapter 6), is exponentially amplified by digital tools that standardize their operations and allow for real-time reporting.

a. The NMBA Mobile Application

This custom application, utilized by MVs and partner NGOs, transforms grassroots activities into structured data points. Its functions include:

- **Geo-tagging and Mapping:** MVs can geo-tag high-risk locations, document drug hotspots, and map the locations of outreach events. This provides district administrators with a dynamic, visual map of the local substance use landscape, enabling precision targeting of resources.
- **Standardized Screening Tools:** The app provides MVs with simple, evidence-based screening questionnaires (such as ASSIST or AUDIT derivatives, adapted for local context) to conduct brief, non-clinical interviews, helping them determine the severity of use and the appropriate referral pathway.
- **Resource Directory:** It maintains a comprehensive, up-to-date database of all nearby NMBA-supported IRCAs, DDCs, and support group meeting locations, ensuring the MV can provide actionable, specific information rather than vague advice.

b. Leveraging Self-Screening and Digital Health Quizzes

Online quizzes and self-assessment tools, designed to be engaging and anonymous, allow users to check their substance use patterns against clinical benchmarks. These tools reduce the cognitive and emotional burden of asking for help, often serving as the **pre-contemplation stage catalyst** that moves an individual toward seeking professional support.

9.4 Tele-Counseling and Virtual Aftercare

For a vast country with limited specialist psychiatrists and counselors, **Tele-Counseling** offers a solution for both rural access and urban convenience, especially in the crucial aftercare phase.

a. Bridging the Urban-Rural Divide

A young person in a remote village may lack access to a weekly in-person counseling session, but they often have access to a mobile network. Tele-counseling (via secure video calls or audio calls) ensures continuity of care, which is vital for relapse prevention (Chapter 8).

b. Consistency and Privacy in Aftercare

Post-rehabilitation, the need for consistent follow-up is high. Tele-counseling offers:

- **Enhanced Privacy:** Counseling sessions can be conducted from the privacy of one's home, avoiding the stigma of being seen entering a physical clinic in their local community.
- **Integration with Daily Life:** The sessions fit around work, college, or family commitments, ensuring that the commitment to recovery is integrated into, rather than separated from, normal life.

c. Virtual Peer Support Groups

Technology also facilitates the extension of **Peer and Group Therapy** (Chapter 8). Secure online platforms allow groups of recovering youth to connect regularly, sharing experiences and providing mutual support, which is often difficult to sustain physically due to geographical spread or time constraints. These virtual communities become the long-term, sober peer support required for sustained sobriety.

9.5 The Challenges of Digital Equity and Safety

While technology offers immense potential, its implementation must be cautious and equity-focused:

1. **Digital Literacy and Connectivity:** Campaigns must accompany technological tools with community training to ensure individuals in low-literacy and poor-connectivity zones can utilize them effectively. NMBA MVs play a direct role in overcoming this barrier.
2. **Data Privacy and Confidentiality:** Given the sensitive nature of the information, the NMBA must maintain the highest standards of data security, encrypting all communication and ensuring strict adherence to confidentiality protocols to build and maintain public trust in the system.
3. **Countering Digital Drug Promotion:** As detailed in Chapter 6, youth-led digital advocacy is necessary to counter the sophisticated use of online platforms by drug suppliers. Technology must be used not just for defense, but for active, offensive advocacy against drug promotion.

The NMBA's technology strategy is about using the twenty-first century's most powerful tool, the mobile phone, to place a confidential, immediate, and comprehensive pathway to recovery directly into the hands of every young person in need, ensuring that help is always just a phone call or a click away.

STORY 5

The Pharmacist's Ledger

A Story of Complicity, Conscience, and Redemption

Mahendra Kapoor polished his pharmacy counter each morning with ritualistic precision. Twenty-three years he'd owned MediCare Pharmacy, twenty-three years of being the neighborhood's trusted health guardian. He knew his customers intimately, Mrs. Patel's blood pressure, Mr. D'Souza's insulin, the young mothers' midnight panic over fevered children.

But lately, a weight had settled in his chest. It had a name he resisted speaking: **guilt**.

It began fourteen months ago with **Sameer**, a college student clutching a crumpled prescription for stimulants. The signature looked wrong,slightly off from Dr. Verma's usual script. Mahendra should have called to verify. That was protocol.

But Sameer looked desperate, reminding him of his own son studying in Pune. Business had been slow. The corporate pharmacy down the street was stealing customers.

"₹450," Mahendra said, packaging the pills with trembling hands.

Sameer returned weekly. Then others came,different faces, same desperation, same questionable prescriptions. Word spread through invisible student networks: *MediCare doesn't ask questions.*

The rationalizations came easily. These were good kids under brutal pressure. They'd just go elsewhere if he refused. At least here they got genuine medication, not adulterated substances.

But rationalization was just guilt wearing a disguise.

Rhea changed everything.

Seventeen years old, school uniform still on, hands shaking as she placed cash on the counter. "The pills. The ones for staying awake."

"I need a prescription," Mahendra said without conviction, the same words he'd said to dozens before ultimately relenting.

"Please, uncle. My NEET exam is three months away. My father will kill me if I don't get into medical college. Everyone's using something."

Her eyes were glassy, ringed with exhaustion. Mahendra saw his own daughter **Priya** at seventeen and felt his stomach twist.

"These medications aren't candy. They have side effects. Addiction potential"

"I'll get them somewhere else then. The pharmacy in Andheri doesn't ask questions."

As she turned to leave, Mahendra faced a choice he'd been avoiding for months.

"Wait," he called out. "Sit."

What followed was conversation, not transaction. Rhea was drowning under expectations that felt like water in her lungs. Started with caffeine pills, graduated to prescription stimulants from seniors. They'd seemed miraculous at first,superhuman focus and retention. But side effects crept in: heart palpitations, insomnia requiring more pills, dependency spiraling.

"I'm trapped," she whispered. "I can't study without them anymore. But I can't keep taking them. I'm disappearing, uncle."

Mahendra felt something crack in his chest. He'd been disappearing too, hadn't he? Each compromised sale eroded who he believed himself to be.

He pulled out a pamphlet from beneath the counter, one he'd received from an **NMBA outreach volunteer** weeks ago and nearly discarded. It listed warning signs, helpline numbers, rehabilitation centers. A section addressed pharmacists: legal obligations, criminal liability, their crucial role as gatekeepers.

"There are people who can help you. Real help, not pills." He hesitated. "And I'm calling your parents."

"You can't!" Panic flooded her face.

"They'll be devastated, but not as devastated as at your funeral. Beta, I have a daughter your age. If she was struggling, I'd want someone to tell me."

Rhea's parents arrived within the hour. Her father's initial denial melted at her mother's terrible recognition. They left as a family in crisis but finally facing it.

After they departed, Mahendra sat in darkness behind his counter, surrounded by medicines that could heal or harm. He thought about every questionable sale, every unverified prescription, every ignored warning sign.

The weight in his chest grew heavier with clear-eyed recognition. But there was also painful relief, the relief of finally stopping pretense.

The next morning, Mahendra called **Inspector Malini Rao**, who'd urged businesses months ago to report suspicious activities. He'd dismissed her then, unwilling to be an informant.

Now Rhea's desperate face haunted his sleep.

"Inspector Rao, this is Mahendra Kapoor from MediCare Pharmacy. I need to report... myself."

The confession poured out, compromised sales, other pharmacies operating similarly, his role in a supply chain quietly poisoning community youth.

"Why now?" she asked.

"Because I met a girl who reminded me why I became a pharmacist. To protect health. I'd forgotten that."

The consequences were real: fines, mandatory retraining, monitoring, professional humiliation. Neighbors who'd trusted him for decades looked at him with confusion.

But there was also unexpected grace. An **NMBA volunteer**, retired pharmacist **Mr. Tandon**, offered an opportunity: would Mahendra join their pharmacist awareness program?

"We don't need saints," Mr. Tandon said. "We need honest people who've confronted their failures and chosen differently."

Mahendra attended workshops on identifying forged prescriptions, legal responsibilities, and having difficult conversations. He learned about the broader ecosystem he'd been part of, how casual pharmacy access fed addiction cycles, how compromised sales represented missed intervention opportunities.

He met counselors, recovered addicts, grieving parents, frustrated doctors. Each conversation transformed abstract ethics into concrete human consequences.

Six months later, **Sameer** returned, thinner, older, wary. He placed a four-month sobriety chip on the counter.

"I wanted you to see this. I nearly died. Cardiac arrhythmia during an exam. When doctors asked what I'd been taking, I eventually told them. My parents found out. It was bad."

He paused. "But I got help. And I realized: everyone in the chain convinced themselves they weren't responsible. The student shared pills. The pharmacist meeting a need. Doctors writing loose prescriptions. Everyone passed the buck, and kids like me nearly died in the gap."

"I'm sorry" Mahendra began.

"You should have said no," Sameer agreed. "But I heard you're doing things differently now. Keep this chip. Not as forgiveness,I'm not there yet. But as a reminder that choices behind this counter matter."

The chip lived in Mahendra's pocket, a talisman against forgetting. He touched it when refusing suspicious prescriptions despite customer anger. When business dipped because he'd become "difficult." When ego whispered he was being self-righteous.

He transformed his pharmacy: posters listing addiction warning signs, NMBA resource pamphlets, and clear verification policies. He trained his assistant **Arjun** rigorously, not just how to dispense medicines, but how to recognize red flags, have compassionate conversations, and see their role as health advocates.

"We're not just selling pills," he told Arjun. "We're guardians. Every person trusts us with their health, that trust is sacred."

Two years after Rhea walked into his shop, Mahendra spoke at a school awareness event. The auditorium was filled with students, teachers, and parents. In the third row sat Rhea, now in college studying literature, looking healthier than he'd ever seen her.

"I'm not here as an expert," Mahendra began. "I'm here as someone who made significant mistakes and is trying to do better.

For years, I was part of the problem, convincing myself I was helping when I was enabling harm."

He spoke about pressures pharmacists faced, about rationalizations, about how complicity accumulated in small compromises. Mostly, he spoke about Rhea, who sought pills that would destroy her and instead saved him.

"She reminded me that every interaction is a choice. Every sale is either harmful or healing. The most important words a pharmacist can sometimes say are not 'here's your medication' but 'let me help you find a better way.'"

After his presentation, a sixteen-year-old boy approached: "What if we're already taking things? Is it too late?"

Mahendra crouched to meet his eyes. "It's never too late to ask for help. NMBA helpline, school counselors, trusted adults, resources exist. And if someone in a pharmacy is willing to sell you controlled substances without verification, walk out. Because they're prioritizing profit over your life."

Rhea approached as the crowd dispersed. "Thank you. For refusing me. For calling my parents. For choosing my life over your convenience. I was angry then. But I'm alive now."

"How are you?" Mahendra asked.

"Good days and hard days. Therapy helps. My parents are different, less about expectations, more about connection. I volunteer with the Youth Club now, talking to other students about finding help before you're drowning."

She paused. "You're part of my story. The part where someone finally said no when everyone else was saying yes or looking away. I needed that no. It felt like cruelty then, but it was actually the first real kindness."

Walking home through crisp autumn air, Mahendra felt the weight in his chest lighten. Not disappearing, some guilt was appropriate, a reminder to remain vigilant. But it no longer crushed him.

Twenty-three years as a pharmacist, only the last two truly understanding what that meant. Not just dispensing pills, but standing at a crucial intersection, where medical access met potential abuse, where desperation met intervention opportunity, where one person's choice could alter another's trajectory.

The next morning, he opened MediCare as always. Polished the counter. Organized inventory. Beside the register sat a small frame: Sameer's sobriety chip and a photo from the school event reminders of why he'd changed and what that change had made possible.

A young man entered with a questionable prescription. Mahendra examined it, then picked up the phone to verify, even as the customer shifted impatiently.

"Standard protocol. It'll just take a moment."

The customer huffed, but Mahendra remained unfazed. He'd learned that protecting health sometimes required accepting unpopularity, that doing right often felt harder than doing easy, and that the most important question wasn't "what can I get away with?" but "what kind of person am I choosing to be?"

Behind him, the NMBA poster displayed a simple message: **"Prevention is everyone's responsibility."**

For the first time in years, standing behind his polished counter, Mahendra Kapoor felt he was truly fulfilling that responsibility.

Not perfectly. Not heroically. But honestly.

And perhaps that was enough.

Part IV

The Societal Mandate

(Policy and Future)

CHAPTER 10

Legal Frameworks and Enforcement: Balancing Justice and Health

10.1 The Dual Mandate: Punitive vs. Therapeutic

The policy response to the substance use crisis in India operates under a necessary dualism: the need to **suppress the supply** of illicit narcotics and the simultaneous need to **address the demand** through public health interventions. The legal architecture is primarily defined by the **Narcotic Drugs and Psychotropic Substances Act, 1985 (NDPS Act)**.

While the NDPS Act was framed with the noble intent of deterring large-scale drug trafficking, imposing stringent penalties for commercial quantities, its broad application often creates a conflict. When a young person struggling with addiction is arrested for possession of a small quantity, they are pushed into the criminal justice system, which exacerbates stigma and makes long-term recovery significantly harder, potentially destroying their educational and career prospects. The *Nasha Mukt Bharat Abhiyaan* (NMBA) recognizes this conflict and mandates a policy shift where health and rehabilitation precede punishment for the user, while enforcement remains targeted at the peddler and trafficker.

10.2 Navigating the NDPS Act: User vs. Trafficker

A critical challenge in enforcement is distinguishing between the **person with a substance use disorder** (the patient) and the

organized criminal (the supplier). The NDPS Act differentiates penalties based on the quantity of the substance seized:

1. **Small Quantity:** Possession for personal consumption, attracting lighter penalties (or providing avenues for exemption).
2. **Intermediate Quantity:** Quantities between small and commercial.
3. **Commercial Quantity:** Large quantities indicating trafficking, which attract severe, mandatory minimum sentences.

The issue often arises when small quantities are misinterpreted or when young, low-level users also engage in petty peddling (to fund their own habits) and face the harsh penalties intended for major traffickers. For the youth demographic, the risk of their lives being permanently derailed by a criminal record, rather than being redirected by treatment, is immense. This is where compassionate enforcement and legal awareness become the tools of the NMBA.

10.3 The Gateway to Health: Section 64A

Recognizing that the threat posed by addiction requires a health response, the NDPS Act includes a crucial provision that aligns perfectly with the NMBA's therapeutic focus: **Section 64A.**

Section 64A grants immunity from prosecution to any addict who volunteers for de-addiction treatment at a recognized facility (such as NMBA-supported Integrated Rehabilitation Centres for Addicts or DDCs). The conditions are strict: the person must be an **addict**, they must make a **voluntary submission** for treatment, and they must undergo the **complete course** of treatment.

This section is the law's explicit recognition of addiction as a disease requiring medical intervention. The success of the NMBA is partly contingent upon maximizing the utilization of this provision, ensuring that law enforcement, judicial officers, and the community are universally aware of this "off-ramp" from the justice system into the health system for young, non-violent users.

10.4 Institutionalizing Compassionate Enforcement

Effective legal strategy for NMBA does not mean weakening law enforcement; it means **redirecting its focus and empowering its personnel** to act as initial referral agents for health.

a. Police Training and Sensitization

The NMBA strategy requires mandatory, ongoing training for police personnel, particularly at the district and local levels. This training must move beyond mere legal compliance to cover:

- **De-escalation Techniques:** Handling young people in withdrawal or crisis with empathy and non-coercive methods.
- **The Disease Model:** Understanding that addiction is a chronic brain disorder, not a moral failing.
- **Referral Pathways:** Immediate, standardized procedures for referring arrestees who qualify for Section 64A directly to the NMBA Helpline (14446) or an IRCA, thus prioritizing immediate clinical care over incarceration.

b. Juvenile Justice and Protection

For users who are minors (under 18), the **Juvenile Justice (Care and Protection of Children) Act, 2015 (JJ Act)** takes precedence. The JJ Act mandates that children in conflict with the law, particularly those with substance use issues, be provided care, protection, and rehabilitation. Their cases must be handled by Juvenile Justice Boards (JJBs), which are legally obligated to recommend institutional and community-based treatment under the care provisions of the Act, reinforcing the therapeutic mandate of NMBA.

10.5 Policy Synergy: The NMBA Imperative

The core policy imperative is **synergy**. The legal framework must support the health goals of the Abhiyaan. This requires:

1. **Data Sharing:** Non-confidential trend data from law enforcement (e.g., emerging drug routes, new synthetic substances seized) must be immediately shared with the Ministry of Social Justice and Empowerment and NMBA partners to inform public health warnings and prevention strategies.
2. **Joint Task Forces:** Establishing dedicated, cross-sectoral task forces (Police, Health officials, NMBA Master Volunteers) in high-prevalence districts to conduct coordinated operations: enforcement against large-scale suppliers combined with simultaneous, non-judgmental outreach and treatment camps for the local community.

By diligently applying the provisions of Section 64A and prioritizing rehabilitation under the JJ Act, the legal system transforms from an obstacle to recovery into a powerful, ethical catalyst for positive change in the lives of young Indians.

CHAPTER 11

The Media, Culture, and Normalization: Countering the Glamour

11.1 The Narrative Battleground: The Illusion of Sophistication

The most subtle, yet pervasive, threat to the drug-free movement is the **cultural normalization and outright glamorization of substance use** in mainstream media. Whether in cinema, OTT series, music videos, or social media trends, drugs and alcohol are often portrayed as essential accessories of success, rebellion, or sophistication. This creates a potent **Illusion of Glamour** that directly contradicts the factual, health-based messaging of prevention campaigns. For vulnerable youth navigating identity and social acceptance, this media narrative is often more compelling than a stern warning from an authority figure.

The societal mandate requires us to recognize media and popular culture as the primary **Narrative Battleground** in the fight against addiction. Our strategy must shift from passively reacting to negative portrayal to actively influencing and shaping positive, responsible, and reality-based cultural content.

11.2 Deconstructing the Myth: Cinematic and Digital Influence

The influence of the media on youth behavior is scientifically documented. Studies have shown that exposure to on-screen smoking and drug use increases the likelihood of a young person initiating that behavior.

a. The Cinematic Challenge

In Indian cinema, the 'tortured artist' or 'rebellious hero' often has a dependency, equating substance use with creativity, intensity, or freedom. While disclaimers are legally mandated, they are often brief and easily overlooked. The emotional weight of the scene, the drama, the music, the actor's charisma, overwhelms the factual warning. The NMBA must engage with the film industry to advocate for **responsible portrayal**, focusing on showing the *true arc* of addiction: isolation, degradation, loss of opportunity, and the difficulty of recovery.

b. The Digital Normalization

Social media and micro-content platforms (Instagram, TikTok) pose a more immediate and decentralized threat. Here, peer influence is magnified, and drug use can be normalized through aesthetically pleasing, rapidly consumed content:

- **The 'Party Culture' Aesthetic:** Portrayals of hedonistic parties where alcohol and drug use are prerequisites for fun.
- **Encrypted Communication:** The use of coded language, emojis, and encrypted messaging in digital media to discuss and facilitate substance procurement, bypassing traditional content filters.

Countering this requires not censorship, but the **youth-led digital advocacy** detailed in Chapter 6, empowering youth to create more authentic, appealing content that promotes sober fun and healthy coping.

11.3 A Code of Conduct for Storytellers: Shifting the Narrative

NMBA needs to institutionalize a framework for collaboration with the creative industry, moving from confrontation to shared responsibility. This involves advocating for a **Voluntary Code of Conduct for Storytellers.**

1. **Mandate for the 'Recovery Arc':** If addiction is portrayed, the narrative must, at some point, show the debilitating consequences and, ideally, the path to recovery, highlighting the dignity of seeking help (e.g., calling 14446 or entering an IRCA).
2. **De-glamorizing the Act:** Avoiding close-ups, romantic lighting, or slow-motion shots that aesthetically glorify the act of drug use. The focus should be clinical, not emotional.
3. **Positive Role Models:** Actively promoting and celebrating characters, based on real-life MVs or recovered individuals, who embody resilience, sobriety, and positive engagement as true markers of success and strength.
4. **Amplifying NMBA Messaging:** Leveraging the star power of public figures to disseminate NMBA messaging and helpline numbers (14446) through public service campaigns that are modern, high-production, and culturally resonant.

11.4 Critical Media Literacy: Training the Audience

Ultimately, the most resilient defense is a critically informed audience. Prevention programs (Chapter 5) must integrate **Critical Media Literacy (CML)** into their curricula.

CML training teaches students to:

- **Identify Subtext:** Understand the hidden commercial or ideological messages behind content (e.g., how an alcohol brand sponsors a sports event to link performance with consumption).

- **Question Motivation:** Analyze why a character uses drugs, is it genuine trauma (a mental health issue) or a lazy plot device designed to make them look 'cool'?
- **Filter Reality:** Distinguish between a fictionalized, dramatic portrayal of drug use and the true, non-negotiable health risks.

By empowering youth to become active, critical consumers of media, NMBA creates an internal shield against the pervasive cultural forces that seek to normalize substance abuse, allowing them to reject the illusion of glamour and choose the reality of empowerment.

CHAPTER 12

Vision 2030: Towards a Drug-Free Generation

12.1 The Destination: Defining a Drug-Free Generation

Nasha Mukt Navnirman is not a short-term project; it is a **long-term commitment to a generational transformation**. The year **2030** is set as a strategic milestone to measure the impact of the NMBA and its community partners. A 'Drug-Free Generation' does not imply zero substance use, an unrealistic goal given global societal trends, but rather a significant, quantifiable reduction in *problematic* substance use and the elimination of the crisis as a major public health and developmental roadblock.

The Vision 2030 goal is defined by three measurable, national-level metrics:

1. **Reduction in Prevalence:** A minimum **25% reduction** in the prevalence of Substance Use Disorders (SUDs) among the 10–25 age group compared to the 2019 baseline data, particularly in high-risk categories like opioids and inhalants.
2. **Universal Treatment Access:** Ensuring that **80% of all individuals** identified with an SUD (and who require formal help) have immediate access to an NMBA-supported treatment facility (IRCA/DDC) or the 14446 Helpline within 25 km of their residence.
3. **Zero Stigma Index:** A measurable increase in the community's willingness to openly discuss mental health and addiction,

as quantified by specialized NMBA social-attitude surveys (e.g., a **50% increase** in family members reporting non-judgmental communication).

12.2 Sustaining Momentum: Institutionalizing the Abhiyaan

A campaign risks fading once the initial mobilization energy subsides. The legacy of NMBA must be its **institutionalization**, embedding the strategy into the permanent structures of government and civil society.

- **Permanent NMBA Directorate:** Creating a dedicated, permanent Directorate within the Ministry of Social Justice and Empowerment, with a mandated budget and cross-ministerial coordination powers (Health, Education, Home Affairs). This ensures policy continuity beyond electoral cycles.
- **Mandatory SEL Integration:** Ensuring that the **Life Skills Education (Chapter 5)** framework, including CML, becomes a mandatory, evaluated component of the national school curriculum, thereby creating an automatically self-renewing generation of resilient citizens.
- **MV Network as a Cadre:** Formally integrating the NMBA Master Volunteer network into recognized national youth organizations (NYKS/NSS), offering continued training and certification (Chapter 6) to ensure a perpetual stream of skilled grassroots leaders.

12.3 Research, Innovation, and the National Resilience Fund

The battle against addiction constantly evolves with new synthetic drugs and changing social dynamics. Vision 2030 must prioritize **investment in innovation.**

- **National Drug Research Institute (NDRI):** Establishing an apex body dedicated to:
    - Epidemiological Surveillance: Tracking new psychoactive substances (NPS) and real-time trend shifts (using MV and Helpline data).
    - Localizing Treatment: Conducting clinical trials to develop culturally appropriate, evidence-based treatment and aftercare protocols (e.g., integrating local yoga/mindfulness practices with CBT).
- **National Resilience Fund:** Creating a dedicated, sustained public-private partnership fund to finance **long-term aftercare, relapse prevention programs, and vocational restoration** (Chapter 8, 8.4). This ensures that a young person who completes residential treatment does not return to a void, but to a funded, structured path toward a dignified future.

12.4 The Legacy of Nasha Mukt Navnirman

The *Nasha Mukt Navnirman* initiative is more than a strategy to fight drugs; it is a blueprint for national youth development. It recognizes that every young person who overcomes addiction represents a massive return on investment for the nation, a skilled worker, a stable parent, a contributing citizen.

The movement asks for a final, profound commitment: that every family, every school, every police officer, and every citizen internalizes the philosophy that addiction is a disease of isolation, and **recovery is a phenomenon of community**. By 2030, the vision is to replace the shame of addiction with the pride of recovery, transforming India's vast youth demographic from a vulnerable population into the most resilient, drug-free, and empowered generation in the nation's history. The foundation is laid; the time to build the future is now.

What you can do next >>>

The "One-Page" Strategy for All

- **The NMBA Helpline (14446):** Keep this number saved. It is the single integrated pathway for crisis, counseling, and recovery.
- **Empathy over Judgment:** The book emphasizes that recovery is a "phenomenon of community". Whether you are a parent, teacher, or peer, your primary role is to provide a "safety net" rather than a "punisher"

Conclusion: The Dawn of A New Construction

As we reach the final pages of "Nasha Mukt Navnirman," it is essential to remember that the word Navnirman does not merely mean "change", it signifies a "new construction." We are not just trying to dismantle the dark networks of substance abuse; we are actively building a new social architecture where every young Indian has the resilience to choose life over temporary escapes.

The journey through these chapters has shown us that the drug epidemic is not an invincible force. It is a shadow that retreats when met with the light of collective action, scientific understanding, and radical empathy. We have seen that the solution lies not in isolated government policies alone, but in the hands of the Master Volunteer in a village, the parent who chooses dialogue over distance, and the student who redefines "cool" through leadership and health.

The roadmap laid out in this book, from the "Family Mandate" to the "Institutional First Line of Defense", is now in your hands. But a map is only as good as the traveler who walks the path. The true "Closing Remarks" of this book will not be written here in ink; they will be written in the lives of the thousands of youth who reclaim their potential, the families that heal from the brink of collapse, and the communities that transform from vulnerable hotspots into bastions of resilience.

Our mission is clear: to ensure that the "Demographic Dividend" of India is never traded for a "Demographic Disaster." We stand at the threshold of a future where prosperity is measured not just by GDP, but by the mental and physical well-being of our citizens.

Let this book be a reminder that silence is the greatest ally of addiction, and your voice is its greatest enemy. Whether you are an educator, a policymaker, or a concerned citizen, your role is vital. The "Drug-Free India" we envision is not a distant utopia, it is a reality we are constructing, brick by brick, heart by heart, starting today.

The path is lit. The construction has begun. Let us move forward, together.

Pledge for Nasha Mukt Bharat Abhiyaan

Nasha Mukt Bharat Pledge

I solemnly pledge that I will neither consume nor promote any form of intoxicating substances.

I affirm my commitment to lead a healthy, disciplined, and responsible life, upholding the values of self-control, dignity, and respect for society.

I shall actively spread awareness about the harmful effects of drug abuse and work towards protecting my family, friends, institution, and community from addiction.

I will encourage and support individuals seeking help, promoting compassion instead of stigma.

I dedicate myself to contributing toward a strong, healthy, and prosperous nation by supporting the vision of a Nasha Mukt Bharat.

Jai Hind.

References

Central Bureau of Narcotics. (n.d.). Annual reports and drug law enforcement statistics. Government of India.

Government of India. (1985). Narcotic Drugs and Psychotropic Substances Act, 1985 (as amended).

Ministry of Health and Family Welfare. (n.d.). National Mental Health Programme (NMHP). Government of India.

Ministry of Social Justice and Empowerment. (2018). National Action Plan for Drug Demand Reduction (2018–2025). Government of India.

Ministry of Social Justice and Empowerment. (2020). Nasha Mukt Bharat Abhiyaan (NMBA): Framework and implementation guidelines. Government of India.

National Crime Records Bureau. (n.d.). Crime in India (Latest available edition). Government of India.

National Drug Dependence Treatment Centre, All India Institute of Medical Sciences. (2019). Magnitude of substance use in India: National survey on extent and pattern of substance use in India. Ministry of Social Justice and Empowerment, Government of India.

Press Information Bureau. (n.d.). Press releases on Nasha Mukt Bharat Abhiyaan and national drug helpline (14446). Government of India.

United Nations. (n.d.). Sustainable Development Goals (Goal 3: Good health and well-being).

United Nations Office on Drugs and Crime. (Various years). World drug report. United Nations.

World Health Organization. (2018). Global status report on alcohol and health. World Health Organization.

Youth Substance Use Self-Screening Form

Time Frame: Please answer based on your experiences during the **last three (3) months**.

Instructions

For each statement, tick (✓) the option that best describes your situation:

Score	**Response**
0	Never
1	Once or Twice
2	Monthly
3	Weekly
4	Daily or Almost Daily

Section A: Usage Pattern

1. I have used alcohol, tobacco, or other psychoactive substances.

   ☐ 0 ☐ 1 ☐ 2 ☐ 3 ☐ 4

2. I require more of the substance than before to feel the same effect.

   ☐ 0 ☐ 1 ☐ 2 ☐ 3 ☐ 4

3. I have used substances in potentially risky situations (e.g., driving, exams, isolation, late-night activities).

   ☐ 0 ☐ 1 ☐ 2 ☐ 3 ☐ 4

Section B: Control & Craving

4. I experience strong urges or cravings to use.

☐ 0 ☐ 1 ☐ 2 ☐ 3 ☐ 4

5. I have attempted to reduce or stop using but was unsuccessful.

☐ 0 ☐ 1 ☐ 2 ☐ 3 ☐ 4

6. I spend considerable time thinking about, arranging, using, or recovering from substance use.

☐ 0 ☐ 1 ☐ 2 ☐ 3 ☐ 4

Section C: Impact on Personal & Academic Life

7. My academic/work performance has been negatively affected.

☐ 0 ☐ 1 ☐ 2 ☐ 3 ☐ 4

8. My relationships with family, friends, or colleagues have suffered.

☐ 0 ☐ 1 ☐ 2 ☐ 3 ☐ 4

9. I have missed responsibilities or important commitments due to substance use.

☐ 0 ☐ 1 ☐ 2 ☐ 3 ☐ 4

10. I continue using it despite knowing it may harm my health, career, or future.

☐ 0 ☐ 1 ☐ 2 ☐ 3 ☐ 4

Scoring

Total Score: ______ / 40

Risk Interpretation Guide

0–8 | Low Risk

No significant indicators of dependency. Maintain healthy coping mechanisms.

9–16 | Moderate Risk

Early warning signs present. Consider reducing use and seeking guidance from a counsellor or mentor.

17–24 | High Risk

Pattern suggests harmful use. Professional counselling is strongly recommended.

25–40 | Severe Risk / Possible Dependency

Strong indicators of substance use disorder. Immediate professional evaluation is advised.

Note

This screening tool is adapted from internationally recognized substance use screening frameworks and is intended solely for educational and preventive purposes. It does not constitute a medical diagnosis.

For confidential support, please consult a qualified healthcare professional or counsellor.

www.ingramcontent.com/pod-product-compliance
Lightning Source LLC
LaVergne TN
LVHW022058200926
848481LV00003B/981

9798903426799